A Church **Music Director's** Handbook

VOLUME 1:
Theology, Vision and Team Building

Greg Cooper
Steve Crain
Andy Judd
Mark Peterson

This book is © 2016 Mountain Street Media Inc. Individual chapters are © their authors, used by permission.

THE HOLY BIBLE, NEW INTERNATIONAL VERSION®, NIV® Copyright © 1973, 1978, 1984, 2011 by Biblica, Inc.® Used by permission. All rights reserved worldwide.

"Saved worship is not saving worship" originally appeared as a blog on mountainstreetmedia.com.

"Please manipulate my emotions" and "Should we sing songs from churches whose theology we disagree with" appeared in modified form on the Garage Hymnal blog.

"How did we get here" appeared in an earlier form as an article in *CASE* magazine.

Thanks to David Peterson, Mike Paget and the parish of St Barnabas Broadway, George Athas, Andrew Massey, Curtis Smith, Philip Percival, Rob Smith, Eddy Soh, Dave Parker and Garage Hymnal.

Paperback ISBN 978-0-9925595-6-4

E-Book ISBN 978-0-9925595-7-1

Contents

Introduction 1

CHAPTER ONE: The worship drama 4

CHAPTER TWO: Saved worship is not saving worship 15

CHAPTER THREE: What kind of music does God like? 23

CHAPTER FOUR: What is the role of the Music Director? 33

CHAPTER FIVE: What should a music team culture look like? 39

CHAPTER SIX: Is music ministry really about music? 59

Taking feedback 70

CHAPTER SEVEN: Team building 72

The five dot-points of good feedback 88

CHAPTER EIGHT: Auditions and skill levels 89

CHAPTER NINE: Emotional manipulation 103

CHAPTER TEN: The lessons of history 105

Andy Judd

Introduction

I think that it was during the second song of the night when I really started kicking myself.

Six minutes earlier, right on schedule and with a warm smile (maybe some nerves too?), the song leader had motioned to those of us chatting down the front to stand and start singing with a mid tempo call to praise. I should say up front that my personal taste in music would normally lean elsewhere. But as I heard the congregation behind me in full flight I couldn't help but be moved. Into my Sunday afternoon fog of worldly worries and mild irritations, the voices all around called me to lift my gaze to a dwell for a moment on a simple truth:

We were far away, the blood of Christ has brought us near.

Of course, in my head I already knew all about that. But for those four minutes Christ was front and centre in my mind and my heart. And I wasn't alone.

That's when I started kicking myself. As I started thinking about all the people – friends, family, neighbours – who I wished I had invited to church tonight.

Not that everything had gone perfectly – the volunteer on the sound desk missed a cue or two, and sickness had wiped out our best bass player (whose replacement occasionally brought with him some subprime note choices). Yet these were rare exceptions to an otherwise inconspicuous excellence.

It struck me that the musicians were singing too – their natural ease hard won through hours of rehearsal. Looking around the band, I saw players all at different levels of musicianship. The professional guitarist with his understated authority; the veteran song leader encouraging her young protégé to take the lead for a song; the experienced drummer graciously adapting his kick drum pattern to lock in with a less versatile bass player. It would be hard to imagine any other context in which such different players would share a stage. But all of them were doing the best they could, with what they've got, for God.

It also struck me how much thought must have gone into planning the service. Song after song, the music landed with creativity and pastoral insight, navigating through the mixed emotional landscape of weighty liturgy, a challenging sermon, and some light hearted announcements. If there was room for spontaneity – a little prayer in response, an unforeseen link to the sermon – it was because the service was so well thought out.

Before you ask – yes, I have taken a little artistic licence in the painting of this picture (conflating together the best bits of a couple of great nights). But these *are* real experiences from my real church. More than once recently I have been brought mid song almost to tears – hearing the unison voices of men and women, some weak, some strong, some in tune, some tone-deaf. All praising God together in song.

But mostly, my church is probably a lot like your church: ups and down and way too many rosters.

This book is about chasing a vision, while dealing with the day to day reality – wrangling with flakey guitarists, practising hostage negotiation with the sound guys, and responding to 40 page complaint emails with grace. Oh, the emails. In Garage Hymnal we used to joke that music ministry is 10% music and 90% emails. But it's worth it.

To help us get there, I've enlisted some of the best music ministers around to provide their practical advice on leading a music ministry in your church.

Mark Peterson is music minister at Holy Trinity Adelaide, and the writer of some incredible songs (See Him Coming, Hallelujah to the King of Kings, Highest Place) which are blessing congregations all over the world. (www.markpeterson.com.au)

Greg Cooper works in music ministry as a producer, songwriter, and trainer with EMU Music, and as a researcher with Effective Ministry. Until recently he served as Music Director at Christ Church St Ives in Sydney. Since 2005 he has written songs, recorded and toured with worship band Garage Hymnal, and has also had a number of well received solo releases. (gregcoopermusic.com)

Steve Crain is a veteran music director. He has been ministering at St Barnabas Broadway since shortly after the council of Nicea, and in that role has trained and discipled whole generations of musicians to steward their musical gifts. When not working at Barneys he freelances as a professional guitarist (listen at stevecrainmusic.com) and is available for church music training seminars.

As for me (**Andrew Judd**), in 2004 I was asked to put together the Annual Conference Band for the Sydney University Evangelical Union — which became Garage Hymnal. I'm also an Anglican Minister.

Andy Judd

CHAPTER ONE: The worship drama

I'm going to tell you a story. It's a big story. It's the story of the whole Bible, Genesis to Revelation, creation to new creation, and all of human history in between. It is a worship drama – a story of humans connecting with God. Everything that has ever happened is caught up in this story. And absolutely everyone who has ever lived is a character in it, whether we realize it or not.

That's why this this is also your story. Where you stand in this story of worship will be incredibly important when you finally meet your maker face to face.

And yet we only have a short chapter. So to tell this story we're going to need to take a colossal step back, switch into panorama mode, and try to take in the whole arc of God's narrative in one glance.

Act one: the fall of worship

The story of worship should have begun very differently.

In the beginning, when God created the world, his intention was never to be a distant and impersonal God. The world is not an anonymous gift. We have a maker, and he loves to give us good things. He is not like some distant bureaucracy, providing services to us from a great distance and without any personal connection. God desires that we should know him, and worship him.

I've been using that word – worship – and I probably should take a second to clarify what I meant by it. Worship can mean all sorts of things:

- to take part in a religious ceremony,
- to scream for a celebrity,
- to sing mid tempo Christian music with your hands in the air.

But we're not going to be using it in any of these ways.

Scholars tell us that throughout the Bible to worship is about "engaging with God on the terms that he proposes and in the way that he alone makes possible".[1] We'll unpack more of what that means as the story unfolds, but as a starting point we can say that worship is about connecting with our creator.

One of the Bible's creation accounts describes how he lovingly planted a Garden for our first parents. In that garden he placed a tree, the tree of life.

This was no ordinary tree, of course. To eat from the tree of life would allow the man and woman to live forever. And live good lives, lives of meaning and purpose, lives of thankfulness to their maker for all his good gifts of life and health and safety, power to work, leisure time to rest and all that is beautiful in creation and human relationships.

But there was a problem.

Our first parents, Adam and Eve, did the opposite of worship.

- They were meant to connect with him as he really is, but they bought into lies about who he is.
- They were meant to respect him, but they openly rejected him.
- They were meant to serve him, but they ignored him
- They were meant to obey him, but they disobeyed his life giving commands
- They were meant to be thankful, but they shook their puny fists at him declaring their independence from their maker, forgetting whose air it was they were breathing.

The Bible calls this development "sin". And I like to think of it in terms of songwriting (bear with me on this!). I occasionally write songs. None of my songs are particularly good – but they're *mine*! I think it's right that the creator of a song be credited as the songwriter.

A while ago a friend of mine (who writes much better songs than me) wrote a killer song, played it to a well know pop star, and then that pop star released it under their own name without crediting my friend,

---

1 Peterson, **Engaging with God**, 20.

the true songwriter. He was rightly devastated. It wasn't the money – at a fraction of a cent per stream, most royalty cheques are barely worth cashing – but what was outrageous was the disrespect.

Plagiarism is rotten. And in a small way it helps us understand the kind of disrespect we show to God when we don't acknowledge him as our creator. When we act as if God isn't real, as if we have no creator, as if we are the authors of our own lives. This pretence, this cosmic plagiarism, is the root of sin.[2]

We demonstrate that we are on board with Adam and Eve's sin decision every time we ignore God. Every time we refuse to thank him for his goodness to us. Every time we sin. If Worship is what happens when humans respond rightly to their God, then Sin is the opposite. Independence. Arrogance. And the tragedy of sin is that, like a B grade plagiarist, we rip off someone else's song but our next album shows we're not the genius we pretended to be. We can't even perform it that well. We play our own tune and our own tune turns out to be not so good. I'll admit there are things I've done I'm not proud of. I fail to live up even to my own standards. How about you?

From Adam and Eve onwards, the history of the world is a downward spiral. Disconnected from our maker, cut off from eternal life, we turn on each other. Adam turns on his wife Eve. Their children murder each other. God looks on in despair as all the inclinations of humanity's hearts are evil all the time, and for a moment regrets making humanity.

The situation between us and God seems impossibly broken. God would have been perfectly justified in cutting the cord, cancelling our credit card, and seeing how long we lasted without light food or oxygen. But he didn't.

We will not worship God – but God will not give up on the people he has made. God instead begins to draw a people to him, inviting them to connect with their maker, and once again worship him as he truly is.

---

[2] At the risk of plagiarising an illustration about plagiarism, I should acknowledge I first heard this illustration about plagiarism used by Tim Keller in his wonderful book on *Prayer: Experiencing Awe and Intimacy with God*.

So God chooses to start with one individual. One family. He chooses Abraham, a man of faith, though not a perfect man. And God makes a promise to him: the whole world will be blessed through him. The whole world will worship their maker again: connect with him as he truly is, respect him, serve him, obey him, and be thankful to him.

With Abraham begins a family line with a promise from God, that they will be the prototype of a new worshipping humanity. This promise is passed from father to Son. From Abraham to his Son Isaac, from Isaac to his son Jacob, from Jacob to his Son Joseph. Joseph ends up in Egypt, and it's there the nation of Israel starts growing massively.

And it's there in Egypt that we pause for a moment to meet Moses, a man with a dark secret.

Act two: pilot light

Even though he mixed with the Egyptian elite, Moses was actually a descendant of Abraham, part of the slave class called Israel. Israel had arrived in Egypt a free nation, but regime change had turned their situation upside down. Now they are slaves to Pharaoh, forced to work under appalling conditions and deprived of basic human rights – including the right to worship.

Moses himself knew the injustice of their situation firsthand – he once witnessed an Egyptian beating a fellow Israelite. He killed the Egyptian in hot blood – this was his dark secret – and when the secret got out he was forced to flee the country.

But he is back now, standing petrified in front of the most powerful ruler in the world. He has a message from God: "let my people go, so that they may hold a festival to me in the wilderness".[3] And he delivers it, reluctantly. A power struggle between God and Pharaoh ensues. Pharaoh continues to escalate the situation: ten times he turns up the

---

3 Exodus 5:1. When the command is repeated in Exodus 7:16, 8:1, 8:20 etc. the purpose given is so that they can "serve" (ESV) or "worship" (NIV) God. The Hebrew word (**avad**) covers normal work ("See you later, I'm off to **avad** in the vineyard...") as well as special religious service ("We're off to **avad** at the temple, did you bring the grain offerings?"). From the context, what seems to be meant here is an ongoing commitment to God, not just a single act of worship.

heat, ignoring ten warnings, and enduring nine plagues – the final plague is what secures their release. God warns that at midnight, he will pass over Egypt and bring judgment on the false gods of Egypt. Only those houses who have sacrificed a lamb and put the blood on their doors will be spared: the rest will suffer the loss of their firstborn. This becomes forever remembered as the Passover, because God passed-over the houses of his true worshipping people.

Suddenly God's people are on the run – passing miraculously through the red sea and into the desert. Safe, and free to worship. This is the exodus: when God rescued his people out of slavery.

God's intention is for them to become a nation of priests, the spiritual guides for the whole world, a pilot light for worshipping humanity.

The pilot light is that little flame in a heater or hot water system which is lit first, so as soon as the time comes the rest of the fuel can be quickly ignited.

As God's pilot light for worship, Israel will be a group who will show the rest of the world how to worship. God gives himself to them in the tabernacle, a tent which represents his presence with them.

And he gives them the law. For them worship will not be a once per week ritual. It will be a whole life lived in light of who God is. In thankfulness. In respect. In obedience to his commands: do not murder, do not steal, do not oppress the powerless. And of course, do not worship other gods.

The law is a high standard, but not an impossible standard – it includes provisions for when they fall short. Animal sacrifices had two uses. Not only can they be used to show allegiance and respect for God, but God also lets them use the blood of animals to pay the penalty for their sin. If you became aware that you had sinned, you could confess you sin and then bring a lamb or goat from the flock as a sin offering, take it to the priest and mark the seriousness of the offence by sacrificing it, splashing its blood on the side of the altar.

It might seem like a strange way to connect with God, but that's the thing – the ability to worship is something that God makes possible. True worship can only happen 'on the terms that he proposes and in the way that he alone makes possible'.[4]

And so imperfect humans can once more connect with a perfect God, through the means he generously provides. Worship can continue despite sin.

That's what should have been.

Moses leaves them alone for a minute to go up the mountain and receive God's ten commandments directly to them. "Wait here. And don't do anything I wouldn't do," Moses says. "I'll be back".

But the Israelites get bored. One thing leads to another, and Moses is not even half way down the mountain when they are worshipping, but not worshipping the invisible God who just smashed Pharaoh and brought them out of Egypt. No, they've made up their own pretend gods and given them the credit. They just broke rule number one, which is: whatever you do, do not make for yourselves gods of silver or gods of gold. "Let's make something a little more visible", they thought. The type of god they would like to worship. Tame, domesticated.

Like the gods we invent for ourselves that will never challenge us because they're a figment of our imagination or made up to suit our needs.

Once again, the situation between us and God seems impossibly broken. God is drawing people back to him, inviting us to connect with our maker, worship him as he truly is. His voice is clear. His claim is right. His invitation means life. *God will not give up on the world he has made and the people he loves – and yet still we will not come.*

But again God will not give up on the world he has made, and he will not break his promise to Abraham, to bring the whole world to worship through him.

People think of the Old Testament as all about law, and the New Testament as about grace. God gives all these rules which they have to keep, but they end up breaking them (classic humans), so God has to bring along Jesus and grace and stuff. But really, it was always about grace. On the edge of the promised land, in Moses final speech, he

---

[4] Peterson, *Engaging with God,* 20.

reminds them that (judging by the golden calf incident) they are going to need to keep coming back to God for forgiveness, and relying on his grace as they live in the Kingdom.

That's one of the reasons why God set up the temple. So they could have a place where they could draw near to God, and seek his grace. (While they were wandering around they had a tent, or "tabernacle", but later when things had settled down on Solomon built a more permanent temple in Jerusalem).

The history of Israel from the very start is one of great highs and devastating lows.

- Under Joshua's good leadership, Israel entered the promised land. (But Israel's faithlessness meant they wandered for 40 years first.)
- The Judges led the nation through periods of renewed worship. (But the human frailty of judges like Samson soon saw Israel worshipping other gods.)
- The great leaders David and his son Solomon unified the nation and restored worship in Jerusalem, building the Temple of the Lord. (But their reigns were also marked by moral and spiritual failure: David became an adulterer and murderer, and Solomon abandoned true worship for the gods of his many wives.)
- In the south, Josiah discovered the law and restored right worship for a moment. (But the kings who followed corrupted the nation's worship.)

So, just like the golden calf debacle, Israel kept worshipping the wrong gods, or worshipping the right God but presuming to decide how to worship him. They kept choosing the best bits of all the religions around them, some even sacrificing their own children as burnt offerings to the Gods of those around them.

There is a great lesson here to those of us who are tempted to approach God on our own terms. On what basis do you think God is happy for your worship? What makes you think God is taking your calls? God is not domesticated – we engage with him on his terms, not our own.

Chapter One: The worship drama

Anyway, all through this people began to notice that the national security of Israel was directly tied to whether they were worshipping the living God or had abandoned him to the fake wooden gods of the surrounding nations. Through his prophets God warned that false worship would lead to a destruction of the nation – and the predictions came tragically true … three times over

- In 922 the nation splits internally.
- In 722, two centuries later, the Northern region is captured and exiled by Assyria.
- In 586 Jerusalem is destroyed and many of the Israelites are taken into exile in Babylon.
- 70 years later some straggled back to Jerusalem, but they lived under foreign rulers for most of the next 500 years.

So much for the pilot project.

The situation between us and God seems impossibly broken. God is not willing not give up on the people he has made. But will they come back to him?

Act three: enter the true worshipper

We fast forward now 600 years, to a conversation between a man and a woman at a well. In the town of Samaria, in the heat of the day. You'd expect most respectable people to be sheltering indoors. The man is on a journey, and he strikes up a conversation – "Will you give me a drink?". It's the woman who points out the obvious – we shouldn't be talking.

Not just because he is a man and she is a woman. In the last 500 years, little has changed. God's prototype for worshipping humanity is still hopelessly divided, the names of the empire around them have changed, as the Assyrians give way to the Babylonians, who give way to the Persians, who give way to the Greeks, who give way to the Romans. But still we are far from the vision of a single nation, and even further from the promises to Abraham.

People might have raised an eyebrow because she is a Samaritan woman. A woman of questionable worship habits. The man is a descendant of those who were exiled and returned; the woman is a descendant of those who stayed behind and started their own breakaway worship of God, based on a different mountain, with new ways of worshipping. They even had a version of the Bible with key words scrubbed out and replaced with their new ways of worshipping.

His comeback is strange: *If you knew who I was, you'd be asking me for a drink*, he replies. *And I would have given you living water.*

Again she points out the obvious. *You've got nothing to draw the water.*

And again his comeback is strange: *If you drink this water, you'll be thirsty again. Drink the water I give you and it will become in you a spring welling up into eternal life.*

She asks where she can get this water. He replies *well why don't you ask your husband.*

I don't have a husband, she says.

And that's when she realises she is not just talking to a strange Jew who forgot his bucket.

No you don't. He replies. You have had 5 husbands and… remind me who are you living with at the moment?

Realising that he is a prophet, she changes the subject to worship, and the clash between their cultures. *You know you Jews claim true worship happens in Jerusalem. We worship here.*

And then the man, Jesus, says something remarkable.

Believe me madam, a time is coming when you will worship the Father neither on this mountain nor in Jerusalem. You Samaritans worship what you do not know, we worship what we do know, for salvation is from the Jews. Yet a time is coming and has now come when the true worshipers will worship the Father in Spirit and in truth, for they are the kind of worshipers the Father seeks. God is spirit, and his worshipers must worship in the Spirit and in truth.

But how can this vision of worship come true? A vision of true worshippers, connecting with God not through a temple or a mountain or a priesthood but directly through God's Spirit?

It's a vision picked up in the prophet Jeremiah, and carried through in the book of Revelation. A vision of a return to the tree of life, a restored garden of Eden, where the water of life flows as clear as crystal flowing from the throne of God and the Lamb down the middle of the great street of the city. On each side of the river stands the tree of life, bearing twelve crops of fruit yielding its fruit every month.

How can the impossibly broken relationship with God be repaired? The law was a far lower bar and we tripped even at that. Who could possibly lead such a revival? Jesus seems to be talking about going global, but even the prototype seems to have failed due to human error? What is the truth which unlocks this worship. How do we get there from an impossibly divided pilot nation, and a corrupt religious leadership?

The situation between God and us seems impossibly broken. We are incapable of worshipping God even on the gracious terms he proposes. He calls but we will not come.

And so he comes to us, and offers a sacrifice on our behalf. But it no ordinary lamb whose blood makes amends for our sins. It is the Lamb of God.

Act three, scene two. It's Passover time in the year AD 33. Jesus, along with all observant Jews, is preparing to celebrate God's bringing Israel out of the land of Egypt to worship him. It has been celebrated essentially the same way for thousands of years. But then Jesus does something different.

Jesus says grace, takes the bread and breaks it saying "Take and eat, this is my body. Then he took the cup and when he had given thanks he gave it to them saying "drink from it, all of you. This is my blood of the covenant which is poured out for many for the forgiveness of sins." (Matthew 26:26-29)

We would not worship, but God would not back away from the mess we made.

We would not come, and so Jesus came to us.

We would not obey God, and so Jesus was obedient on our behalf.

We were under a self-inflicted curse, Jesus became a curse for us.

We would not make sacrifice for our sins, and so Jesus offered himself as one sacrifice for all time, on a tree, the cross.

> "He himself bore our sins" in his body on the cross, so that we might die to sins and live for righteousness; "by his wounds you have been healed." (1 Peter 2:24)

Our own priests had failed us, so he became a great high priest.

Our own temple was corrupt, so he made his body a temple

Our own kings had failed to lead us to worship God, so he became a human king.

There really is only one true, saving worship. There is one true worshipper. Jesus Christ. Any other worship is useless. Worse than useless, in fact, it's idolatry.

But there is more to this story. Because through the *saving worship* of Christ we are invited to take part in the *saved worship* of his people.

Andy Judd

CHAPTER TWO: Saved worship is not saving worship

Here's a big claim: I think that almost all the most serious problems we run into when it comes to church gatherings have to do with a confusion between **saving** worship and **saved** worship.

Jesus' saving worship

Sav*ing* worship is the worship that saves us.

You may have experienced in your own life how easily malice and disrespect can break a relationship. The gospel tells us that humanity's continual disrespect towards our maker has damaged our relationship with him. Saving worship is about making that relationship right again – making peace with God.

The thing is, nothing we do can fix this relationship. God must make the first move. Saving worship can only happen on God's initiative, by his grace. There is only one example of saving worship that works, and that is the worship performed by Jesus on our behalf.

Let's have a look at Hebrews 10:8-14. The first thing to note is that human actions (even worship offered in accordance with the Old Testament law) cannot save us:

> First he said, "Sacrifices and offerings, burnt offerings and sin offerings you did not desire, nor were you pleased with them" — though they were offered in accordance with the law.
> (Hebrews 10:8)

Our attempts to obey God do not cut it. That's the first thing, and it's the bad news. But there is a second thing, and it's good news:

> Then he said, "Here I am, I have come to do your will." He sets

> aside the first to establish the second. ¹⁰ And by that will, we have been made holy through the sacrifice of the body of Jesus Christ once for all. (Hebrews 10:9-10)

The gospel tells us that what humanity was unwilling and unable to do, God sent Jesus to do on our behalf:

> Day after day every priest stands and performs his religious duties; again and again he offers the same sacrifices, which can never take away sins. ¹² But when this priest [Jesus] had offered for all time one sacrifice for sins, he sat down at the right hand of God, ¹³ and since that time he waits for his enemies to be made his footstool. ¹⁴ For by one sacrifice he has made perfect forever those who are being made holy. (Hebrews 10:11-14)

Jesus' sacrifice on the cross is the only sav*ing* worship. Nothing that we do in church, nothing that we do in our lives, can make us right with him. Our good deeds do not cut it. Our prayers do not reconcile us. Our church services do not win him over. The only true saving worship is that performed by Jesus, which is why:

> "Salvation is found in no one else, for there is no other name under heaven given to mankind by which we must be saved." (Acts 4:12)

Our saved worship

Sav*ed* worship is the worship we can do once we are saved, and in response to Jesus' sacrifice.

You might be wondering why then we keep using worship language to talk about things in the Christian life? Why do we have *worship* music? Church *services*? Why collect *offerings* of gifts for the poor? Surely this risks suggesting that our actions are able to make us acceptable to God?

The answer is simple. We talk about Christian life as worship because the writers of the New Testament do. For instance in Acts 13:

> While they [the early church] were **worshiping** the Lord and fasting, the Holy Spirit said, "Set apart for me Barnabas and Saul for the work to which I have called them." (Acts 13:2)

But the difference between our worship and Jesus' worship is that our worship is not sav*ing* worship. It's sav*ed* worship.

Sav*ed* worship is the worship you can do *once you're already saved*. It doesn't make you right with God. And our saved worship (music, service, offerings etc) is only acceptable to God on the basis of Jesus' saving worship:

Our saved worship must follow Jesus' saving worship.
It can only follow Jesus' saving worship.
And it always follows Jesus' saving worship.

Let's have a look at these examples of saved worship in the New Testament.

1. Saved worship includes love, hospitality and visiting prisoners

Hebrews 12 talks about what happens once we are saved:

> Therefore, since we are receiving a kingdom that cannot be shaken, let us be thankful, and so *worship* God acceptably with *reverence* and *awe*, for our "God is a consuming fire."
> (Hebrews 12:28-29)

See all those worship flavoured words? Worship, reverence, awe … they all follow the "therefore". They are only possible because we've already received the benefits of Christ's saving worship.

Then, having spoken about "serving God acceptably with reverence and fear", the writer to the Hebrews goes on to give some specific examples of what a lifestyle of worship might look like.

> Let brotherly love continue. ² Don't neglect to show hospitality, for by doing this some have welcomed angels as guests without knowing it. ³ Remember the prisoners, as though you were in prison with them. (Hebrews. 13:1-3)

So our *saved* worship will include specific acts of love for those in need. These can happen anywhere, including (but not only) when the church meets together.

2. Saved worship includes collections for the needy

In several places, the apostle Paul describes the collection of money for the poor by a church as a type of worship. I have put the worship language in bold:

> Right now I am traveling to Jerusalem to **serve [Greek: diakonon]** the saints, ²⁶ for Macedonia and Achaia, were pleased to make a contribution for the poor among the saints in Jerusalem. ²⁷ Yes, they were pleased, and indeed are indebted to them. For if the Gentiles have shared in their spiritual benefits, then they are obligated to **minister [Greek: leitourgeo, meaning to do a work for the people in a civic or religious context]** to Jews in material needs. (Romans 15:25-27)

> Now the One who provides seed for the sower and bread for food will provide and multiply your seed and increase the harvest of your righteousness. ¹¹ You will be enriched in every way for all generosity, which produces thanksgiving to God through us. ¹² For the ministry of this **service [Greek: leitourgia, meaning worship or service in a sacrificial system]** is not only supplying the needs of the saints, but is also overflowing in many acts of thanksgiving to God. ¹³ They will glorify God for your obedience to the confession of the gospel of Christ, and for your generosity in sharing with them and with others through the proof provided by this **service [Greek: diakonia, meaning service or ministry]**. (2 Corinthians 9:10-13)

> But I have received everything in full, and I have an abundance. I am fully supplied, having received from Epaphroditus what you provided—a fragrant offering, an acceptable **sacrifice [Greek: thusia]**, pleasing to God. (Philippians 4:18)

3. Saved worship includes praising God

Whether in church gatherings or outside, sung or said, praise of God is described as a type of sacrifice, alongside sharing with others:

> Therefore, through Him let us continually offer up to God a **sacrifice [Greek: thusia]** of praise, that is, the fruit of our lips that confess His name. [16] Don't neglect to do what is good and to share, for God is pleased with such **sacrifices [Greek: thusia]**. (Hebrews 13:15-16)

4. Saved worship includes Christian ministry

Paul describes his own work as an apostle in sacrificial terms:

> My brothers, I myself am convinced about you that you also are full of goodness, filled with all knowledge, and able to instruct one another. [15] Nevertheless, I have written to remind you more boldly on some points because of the grace given me by God [16] to be a **minister [Greek: leitourgos, meaning someone who serves]** of Christ Jesus to the Gentiles, **serving as a priest [Greek: hierourgeo, meaning to act as a priest]** of God's good news. My purpose is that the **offering [Greek: prosphora]** of the Gentiles may be acceptable, sanctified by the Holy Spirit. (Romans 15:14-16)

We have to be careful here. Paul is not saying that he is an actual priest in the sense of *saving* worship – he is definitely not mediating between the people and God or performing sacrifices on their behalf. That would undermine the whole message he is bringing to them about Jesus! What Paul means is that by preaching the gospel he enables people to hear about Jesus and his saving worship, and then once they are saved they can offer *themselves* as saved worship, 'living sacrifices' (12:1). Paul's worship ministry takes the specific forms of evangelism, preaching and prayer (Rom 1:8-15)

5. And (of course) saved worship includes our whole lives

As well as the specific acts seen above, the Bible speaks about our whole lives as saved worship.

> Therefore, I urge you, brothers and sisters, in view of God's mercy, to offer your bodies as a **living sacrifice [Greek: thusia]**, holy and pleasing to God—this is your true and proper **worship [Greek: latreia]**. (Romans 12:1)

As a side note, some people have suggested that we should *only* talk about worship in this "whole of life" way, and that we should therefore not talk about church services as worship at all. This might help some people avoid talking about church as if it's the only real type of worship (which as we've seen it is not!), but in doing so it risks making the opposite mistake: it implies that church is the one sphere of life where we *do not* worship God! It's as if we can worship anywhere we like – on the bus, at home, at work – as long as it's not in church.

If we can't talk about church as worship then, as Don Carson points out, we lose one very important way of speaking about our church gatherings:

> "if one uses the term worship only in its broadest and theologically richest sense [i.e. as all of life], then sooner or later one finds oneself looking for a term that embraces the particular activities of the gathered people of God described in the New Testament. For lack of a better alternative, I have chosen the term corporate worship — but I recognise the ambiguities inherent in it" (D. A. Carson, "Worship Under the Word", in **Worship by the Book**, 49).

Saved worship is not sav*ing* worship

The Bible's picture of saved worship is much much bigger than most people realise.
- Saved worship is a general attitude of life *and* in specific acts.
- Saved worship can be done as individuals *or* as a church gathered together.

And yet none of this worship makes us right with God. God doesn't hear us because of our musical excellence, or even our sincere hearts. When a relationship is broken by disrespect, even otherwise nice things become soured (the kiss of an unrepentant adulterer makes the innocent party flinch at its insincerity). So it is with our worship if we are not reconciled with God:

> All of us have become like one who is unclean,
> and all our righteous acts are like filthy rags; (Isaiah 64:6)

Without Christ's *saving* worship, our songs are not the kind of music God wants to hear.

Without Christ's *saving* worship, our prayers are not acceptable to God. God doesn't hear us because of the length or passion or wording of our prayers.

Without Christ's *saving* worship, our lives are not an acceptable sacrifice to God. God does not love us because of our good works or our right behaviour or our standing in society.

These works are filthy rags, except through Jesus' saving worship.

Further reading

David G. Peterson. *Engaging with God* (IVP, 2002).

BIBLICAL WORDS FOR WORSHIP

There is no one word for worship in the Bible. In fact, there are three groups of ideas which have a worship flavour, and each of them conveys a different aspect of the broader idea of worship.

To bow
Hebrew: hishtahweh
Greek: proskuneo

To bow the knee in adoration, expressing submission to him and grateful recognition of who he is.

To serve
Hebrew: avad
Greek: leiturgeo

To serve him obediently both in specific acts and generally in life.

To fear
Hebrew: yara
Greek: phobeo

To show reverence or respect for God in every aspect of life.

Andy Judd

CHAPTER THREE: What kind of music does God like?

You only have to be involved in music ministry for ten minutes to realise that everyone has an opinion on the music we sing in church. For starters, people feel strongly about music in general, and we all have different tastes in music (my wife Steph is an Opera singer and I am a Jazz Pianist… it may not surprise you that sometimes we disagree on what we'd like to listen to over dinner). But when it comes to church music the stakes are raised even higher. Everyone has their own rules about church music.

I'm sure I've heard it all. No drums. No drum sticks. No ride cymbals. No swaying. No standing in the middle of the stage. No standing on the stage. No calling the 'stage' the 'stage'. No singlets. No shorts. No unenclosed shoes. No smiling. No closing eyes. No raising hands past the elbow. No microphones. No sharp keys. No flat keys. No describing worship music as worship. No talking during songs. No songs during talking. No guitar solos. Never more than two songs in a row. No more than two bars intro. No 'I' songs. None of *your* songs. No Hillsongs. Nothing but Hillsongs…

I remember sending my band off to a gig at a church I couldn't be at. The report came back that the church was unhappy. Why, what was wrong? "Well… the drummer didn't wear pants … and the singer closed her eyes." (I had to read that email a few times before I realised the two issues weren't connected.)

Everyone has their own opinion about church music. But whether we realise it or not, most of us have a sneaky habit of bringing in theology to justify our opinions on everything from the tunes we sing to which instruments are allowed and what musicians should wear on stage. God's taste in music often sounds suspiciously like our own.

So I want to ask a different question. What is God's taste in music? And I want to start with Colossians 3:15-17:

> Let the peace of Christ rule in your hearts, since as members of one body you were called to peace. And be thankful. Let the message of Christ dwell among you richly as you teach and admonish one another with all wisdom through psalms, hymns, and songs from the Spirit, singing to God with gratitude in your hearts. And whatever you do, whether in word or deed, do it all in the name of the Lord Jesus, giving thanks to God the Father through him.

Somewhere on their body, every Music Director should have a tattoo of Colossians 3:16-17. Either that or Ephesians 5:15-20:

> Be very careful, then, how you live —not as unwise but as wise, making the most of every opportunity, because the days are evil. Therefore do not be foolish, but understand what the Lord's will is. Do not get drunk on wine, which leads to debauchery. Instead, be filled with the Spirit, speaking to one another with psalms, hymns, and songs from the Spirit. Sing and make music from your heart to the Lord, always giving thanks to God the Father for everything, in the name of our Lord Jesus Christ.

I think these verses give us a great place to start thinking about what kind of music God likes.

1. Music that's all about Jesus

> Let the message of Christ dwell among you richly...
> (Colossians 3:16)

My brother works in the media. He's often doing interviews with important people about important things. And one thing that ruins an important interview is a bonehead.

A bonehead is a technical expression. It refers to that person who, seeing a television crew doing an interview with someone, can't help themselves. They simply must get in the background of the shot and put the bunny ears over the head of the interviewee.

It doesn't matter how life and death serious the interview is. It could be the fire chief telling people to evacuate their homes or face certain death – it doesn't matter to a bonehead – they simply must get in the background of the shot and distract the viewers at home, waving to their mum, making silly gestures, generally looking like an idiot. That's a bonehead.

And chances are, if you're anything like me, you're tempted to be a bonehead all the time. There I am on stage at a Christian conference singing about Jesus, the eternal second person of the Godhead, the incarnate saviour of all humanity, who defeated death and now reigns over the universe… and all the time I'm thinking about myself. "Look how awesome I am playing this song. I wonder if people are noticing."

Seriously?

You think you're impressive… next to *Jesus???*

Bonehead.

Whatever we are doing, it needs to be about Jesus. Not us. It is the "message of Christ" that is front and central in our music. Everything else must serve that message, or move aside.

Now, I think everyone is capable of being a bonehead from time to time. It may surprise you (maybe not!) to learn that many preachers struggle with the same thing. The best remedy I've found is, when you catch yourself doing it, to laugh at yourself. Jesus will forgive us for thoughtlessly attempting to steal his glory, but it's awfully embarrassing to realise how lame we must look doing it!

2. Music of the heart

> … singing to God with gratitude in your hearts (Colossians 3:16)

> … Sing and make music from your heart to the Lord (Ephesians 5:19)

Here's the thing, God has heard a lot of empty worship in his time. And he isn't really looking for more of it. When the message about Christ is dwelling in us richly, it is only natural that we respond by with music *in* and *from* our hearts. The point is not that we should be singing silently (as if he means *only* in our hearts), but that we should be singing with our whole being. That includes our head, our hearts … yes, maybe even our hands (Steve Crain reckons our *hips* as well).

James 5:13 makes a direct connection between our joy and our singing:

> [13] Is anyone among you in trouble? Let them pray. Is anyone happy? Let them sing songs of praise.

Some people are afraid of expressing emotion in church because it can be false. We talk more about that in **chapter x.** And sure, not everyone is as in touch with their emotions or expresses emotion in the same way (it's OK, God still loves you Anglicans). But I do think to not ever be moved by anything we sing about in church is a great shame. And to make music which encourages people to sing about Jesus while thinking about what's for dinner is probably worse than not having music at all.

3. Music which is excellent teaching

> As you teach and admonish one another with all wisdom
> through psalms, hymns, and songs from the Spirit,
> (Colossians 3:16)

I used to do a lot of music ministry, but truth is these days I spend most of my time as a pastor and preacher. And here's something I've noticed:

People pay far more attention to the songs than the sermon.

There, I said it. (You probably shouldn't tell this to you preaching team – it might make them sad and angry.)

Case in point: the other day we introduced a song to our congregation. At least half a dozen people raised serious theological concerns about the song with me and other members of the staff team. People were very concerned that one of the lines contained a misleading theological statement.

The thing is, the exact same lines had been used in a recent sermon. The exact same idea, expressed in the exact same words. I know this because I wrote the sermon and co-wrote the song.

This drove home an important lesson to me – people can snooze through a sermon, but the songs put words into their mouth and thoughts into their hearts. Nobody has ever recited my sermons as they make their morning coffee (as far as I know). But a good song can stay with people throughout the week.

Longer than that, even. My grandfather has cognitive dementia. He can't always tell you what his name is. But he can still sing all the verses of *In Christ Alone*.

So the goal cannot be simply to have songs which are 'not heretical'. That's a stupidly low bar. We need songs that nourish our souls with the word of Christ: *richly*, not *passably*. We need songs that teach and admonish, not just feel good to sing. We need songs that contain all the wisdom we have access to in Christ, not just the clichés that fill in space.

4. Music which is excellent music

> And whatever you do, whether in word or deed, do it all in the name of the Lord Jesus ... (Colossians 3:17)

Here's the thing though – as soon as I say that our music needs to be excellent theology, I need to make sure we're all on board with this as well: to be an excellent song, it has to also be excellent music. The words and the tune are not incidental to each other. They both work together to create the meaning.

And so the music I think should be excellent.

By excellent, I don't mean that every piano player needs to outshine Bill Evans. I mean we need to be aiming to do the best we can with what we've got. How else should we go about making music 'in the name of the Lord Jesus'? Sloppily? Apathetically? Bad music just doesn't fit the genre.

You only have to watch a sunrise to realise that the creator cares about beauty. It's fitting that we play our instruments skilfully at all times, but particularly when we are praising him:

> ² Praise the Lord with the harp;
> make music to him on the ten-stringed lyre.
> ³ Sing to him a new song;
> play skillfully, and shout for joy. (Psalm 33:2-3)

5. Music with a mission

> Be very careful, then, how you live — not as unwise but as wise, making the most of every opportunity, because the days are evil. (Ephesians 5:15)

Church is the gathering of God's people. But it is also a way that the message about Christ is shared with the world. Think about Paul and Silas in Acts 16:25 — they are in prison, singing to God, *and the other prisoners are listening to them*. (That's presumably how the gaoler knows who they are and who they believe in later when the Lord breaks them out of prison.)

I once played at a church where the legendary evangelist John Chapman was attending. Before the service he asked me what type of music we were planning on playing. It's fair to assume that he and I, though we shared much unity in the gospel, shared very little of our music tastes. He had heard us sound-checking and he feared the worst.

"I'm afraid it'll be the kind of music you don't like, Chappo."

"Well then Brother" – that's what he called anyone whose name he couldn't remember – "how do you go about choosing what style of music to play?"

"Well, Chappo, we have a think about the non Christian people we're trying to reach in this area, and think about what kind of music will make sense to them, and then we play that."

Chappo smiled warmly. "Good on you, then, Brother."

I'll never forget that morning.

6. Music by the Spirit

> Do not get drunk on wine, which leads to debauchery. Instead, be filled with the Spirit, speaking to one another with psalms, hymns, and songs from the Spirit ... (Ephesians 5:18-19)

There is a choice. We can be controlled and influenced by things which are bad for us, like too much wine, false teachings, or parts of our culture which oppose God. *Or* we can be controlled and influenced by the Spirit. I long for our meetings to be more and more moved and empowered by the Holy Spirit, and I suspect you do too.

But people have different ideas about what it looks like for the Spirit to show up. Some people think that certain gatherings are more Spiritual because they are more spontaneous, whereas others are less Spiritual because they care more about theology. It seems we have to pick either Spirit or Truth – one or the other, but not both.

But the call to 'Spirit-inspired' singing in Colossians 3:16 and Ephesians 5:19 is not particularly a comment for (or against) spontaneity, but is about who inspires the psalms, hymns and songs.[5] Whether truth about Jesus becomes clear in a moment during a service, or over decades of careful meditation on Scripture, it is only the Spirit of God who can reveal Christ to us.

Remember the Samaritan woman at the well in chapter 1 (act three of the worship drama) – Jesus told her that true worshippers will worship in Spirit and in Truth. These aren't in tension. "Spirit and Truth" do not have terribly much to do with whether our music is well rehearsed or spontaneous. Nor does the phrase mean simply that we should aim for right knowledge, as well as right motives. Spirit and Truth go together. Jesus *is* the truth (John 14:6). And *his Spirit* makes our worship possible

---

[5] By the way, Peter O'Brien doesn't think it's possible to distinguish very sharply between 'psalms', 'hymns' and 'songs' (***The Letter to the Ephesians***, 395). And if Peter O'Brien can't work out the difference, I'm certainly not game to try.

by showing us who Jesus is, and enabling us to recognise and respond to him as he really is.

Trinitarian music will always point us to Jesus. Notice how all three members of the Godhead are involved in Colossians 3:16:

> Let the **message of Christ** ... through psalms, hymns, and songs **from the Spirit,** singing **to God** ... in the name of the **Lord Jesus**, giving thanks to **God the Father** through **him.**

Some people think that to be properly Trinitarian is to alternate verses between Father, Son and Spirit. These songs are often awful. And often they're not even Trinitarian – we don't have three Gods who we have to give equal air time to. We have one God who reveals himself as he really is: three persons who share one being, and who always work together, in perfect unity and ordered distinction. So Peter O'Brien points out that if we're really singing in the Spirit then actually most of the time we'll be addressing our songs to 'Christ' or 'God' (and each other). So in our songs, I expect normally we'll be singing about what God (Father, Son and Spirit) has done in Jesus:

> ... Christians filled by the Holy Spirit give thanks to God the Father on the basis of who Jesus is and what he has accomplished for his people by his death and resurrection. (O'Brien, 398)

Not surprisingly, this is the way most of the songs in the New Testament seem to go (Philippians 2:6-11, Colossians 1:15-20, 1 Timothy 3:16, Revelation 5:9, 5:13, 7:10, 12:10).[6]

7. Music which is about other people

> Let the peace of Christ rule in your hearts, since as members of one body you were called to peace. And be thankful. Let the message of Christ dwell among you richly as you teach and admonish one another with all wisdom through psalms, hymns, and songs from the Spirit ... (Colossians 3:15-16)

---

6 *The Letter to the Ephesians*, 396.

In Colossians 3:16 (and in Ephesians 5:19) the singing happens simultaneously in two dimensions: we are teaching and admonishing 'one another', at the same time as singing 'to God'. It's a mistake to think about church music as *only* a time for you personally connecting with God. But it's also a mistake to think of church music simply as Christian karaoke (something we do for our own amusement) or as a memory aid (something we do to help each other learn things about God). It's about God, *and* about other people.

I think that means you'll want to think carefully about how helpful your award winning rendition of Bach's Cantatas or your 'out' Jazz reharmonisation of Amazing Grace is … if the church is full of people who don't have any cultural connection or understanding of those musical genres.

Singing is something we do together. That doesn't mean that there is never any place for performance items or instrumental bridges or times of personal reflection. The point is that, like absolutely everything in church, the idea behind any music must be to build up the church:

> What then shall we say, brothers and sisters? When you come together, each of you has a hymn, or a word of instruction, a revelation, a tongue or an interpretation. Everything must be done so that the church may be built up. (1 Corinthians 14:26)

The technical term for this is edification – but edification in this context means more than just "feeling great afterwards". It means weak Christians encouraged, immature Christians challenged, and new Christians turned to God.

I think I learnt the most about this kind of music from some old people in a small church somewhere in country Queensland. We were on a tour and had been asked to lead the singing at their morning service. As we played our songs and led the congregation I could tell that the oldies up the front were not, shall we say, on board. For starters, it was obvious from their body language that it was way louder than they liked (this was exacerbated by the cruel irony of church life that most old people sit diligently up the front while the young people sit far up the back further from the speakers.)

Afterwards, one of them came up and said those awful ten words, the ones feared by music directors the world over:

"I would like to talk to you about the music."

You know the drill. I tensed instinctively, assumed a resigned though deferential posture and loaded up my active listening skills. But what he wanted to say stunned us all.

"I just want to say how much we appreciate you coming in today, and how good it is to see all these young visitors up the back who we've never seen before. It's great to know that when we're long gone and buried, there will be people here to carry on the work in this church."

> Let each of you look not only to his own interests, but also to the interests of others. (Philippians 2:4)

I hope when I'm his age, and the kids are playing terrible music far too softly, that I can have his same attitude. Because I'm convinced *that's* the kind of music God likes.

Further reading

Peter T. O'Brien, *Colossians, Philemon*. Word Biblical Commentary. Thomas Nelson, 2000.

Peter T. O'Brien, *The Letter to the Ephesians*. Pillar New Testament Commentary. Eerdmans, 1999.

Greg Cooper

CHAPTER FOUR: What is the role of the Music Director?

Music Director. It's a role that has considerable history in churches worldwide but in Australian churches has emerged only fairly recently. It's exciting to see churches formalising this role - in either a paid or unpaid capacity. The indication is that churches are keen to invest energy, time, and resources into the area of music ministry, aware of the impact of church singing on church life. Those of us with a heart for music in churches can't help but be encouraged by this development.

However, once you scratch a little below the surface, it seems that although often well intended, the role of Music Director is perhaps misunderstood or ill-defined in many church settings. Too often, the exact scope and goals of the role are not well established upfront. And the role can easily be reduced to doing whatever is necessary to 'make music on Sundays happen'.

It's easy to see why this happens! After all, it's a role with many dimensions. While no one Music Director will be able to do all these things with equal strength, the role can involve jobs such as selecting music for church gatherings, shaping bands, rostering people, leading bands, leading singing, overseeing tech teams, sourcing and maintaining PA systems, training musicians, and engaging with members of the congregation on music issues - just to name a few.

These are all really important jobs that need to get done. But simply 'making music on Sundays happen' is a deficient goal – because in one way or another, the music will happen. It might be terrible, but it will happen. With this kind of a goal, the Music Director can often go home on a Sunday night feeling strangely unsure as to whether they have actually done their job well or not.

We need to aim for more than that. Not for our own egos. Not to look impressive. But to do our best to handle well God's Word in song, and to care well for God's people in the church. And that means thinking carefully about what our goal is as a Music Director. Focusing merely on 'making music happen' means something else will get forgotten. Something that is very, very important. As American writer Todd Henry suggests,

> "we often confuse short-term efficiency with long-term effectiveness. This means that we fail to do the very things that will add disproportionate value in the long term while continuing to labor over short-term activities that give us a sense of forward progress, but ultimately rob us of our unique, valuable contribution." (Todd Henry, *Louder Than Words*, p159)

A suggested main role: creating culture

Being a Music Director is a leadership role. I want to suggest that the main role of a Music Director is to lead by creating a culture within a church where music ministry can flourish. This current of culture is unseen, but can help grow disciples in their love and knowledge of God.

By culture, I simply mean the ideas and behaviours of a group. When it comes to church music culture, there are two elements to consider: the culture of the church (ie, congregations), and the culture of the music team.

The culture of the church is the direct responsibility of the Senior Minister (or Rector or Pastor) and not the Music Director - but there is very much a joint effort required from these two people. You could perhaps say it is an indirect responsibility of the Music Director. The Music Director is responsible for helping the Senior Minister think through aspects of this culture.

The culture of the music team is the direct responsibility of the Music Director. Ephesians 4:12 suggests that it is a pastor's role to prepare or equip God's people for works of services (i.e., ministry).

Even if a Music Director is not seen as a pastor, the roles do share some functions - leading a team, caring for them, praying for them, and speaking the Word of God into people's lives. To this extent, then, it is the Music Director's role to prepare and equip the music team for their ministry. So rather than the Music Director doing all the work themselves, they help to equip a team to share and carry out the work together. Creating a team culture is a powerful way to do this.

How can we create a music team culture?

Where there are people, there are cultures. Groups of people will form a culture whether asked to or not. So a culture can emerge either unintentionally or intentionally.

Unintentional culture

A music team culture may emerge unintentionally and end up being exactly the culture you hoped for. Everyone serves well, looks after their spiritual health, and has high levels of musicianship of their own accord. Amazing!

But let's be honest - that is unlikely! More often than not, a culture that forms unintentionally will require leadership to step in and course-correct the current of the culture. Think of a political party where leadership is weak, and the party is seen to have 'lost its way'... This is not the culture we want! What we want is an intentional culture.

Intentional culture

An intentional culture emerges when a clear set of values is established, communicated, and practised. This requires leadership to:
- establish the values that you want to see in your team;
- communicate those values clearly and regularly; and
- practise (and model) those values.

We'll discuss particular values in the next chapter.

A well functioning culture is, in my view, a thing of beauty! Sound over the top? Well, hear me out.

The cafe model

I love coffee. And you might just too. So let's try and relate this to coffee.

Think about a cafe that has excellent customer service, clean tables, a welcoming, relaxed vibe, and great coffee. The presence of these things is not a coincidence. The management will have set out clear values, communicated them to their staff, and helped them to practise them.

When you are in one of these cafes, you see the smoothness with which the place runs, and the way in which the wait staff seem to be on the same page in how they operate. It's as though the cafe has always been like this, and could never have operated any other way.

But you need only walk in to a poorly run cafe to instantly detect that cafes can very much exist in other (and less effective) ways. You realise that you feel uneasy in this second cafe. The service is average - you have to chase up your order. The environment is not peaceful. And staff members are not welcoming. You leave feeling unsettled. And you realise that there must be reasons why you felt good in the first cafe…

I believe this is because the culture in the good cafe was carefully thought through and well practised. You barely noticed the details of the cafe environment, because they didn't impact negatively on your experience. You were able to focus on enjoying your food and your conversation. The cafe just worked well! You left feeling refreshed. In the poorly run cafe, however, it was very difficult to focus on your food and your conversation, because you were constantly distracted by the uneasiness of the surroundings.

Church music team culture is a bit like a cafe culture

OK, so as great as coffee is, come back with me to the church setting. Cafes create a culture where dining can happen effectively. As music leaders, we should aim to create a church music culture where congregational singing can happen effectively, so that people leave church focusing not on the band or the singers or the things that went wrong, but on the saving grace of the Lord Jesus Christ, and his lordship over every aspect of their lives.

If you are a Music Director reading this, you may be thinking that the idea of working primarily on culture is a complete luxury. You're too busy getting rosters done, song leading and band leading, selecting songs for Sunday, and, well, just keeping your head above water.

Now, don't get me wrong - those are all important things that have to happen!

But I believe that when the right culture exists, those things will happen. No, they won't happen magically without human effort. But they will happen.

You will be directly involved in making *some* things happen - but not all things.

Members of the music team will co-own the vision for the music ministry alongside you.

You will not feel the burden to make all these things happen on your own. They will happen as a matter of course.

You will be able to step back at the right times to see the bigger picture.

You will be able to focus on caring for the Christian growth of people in the music team and the congregation.

And importantly, the members of your music team will be focused on the right things - they will have a clear sense of purpose.

What's at stake here?

Why does this culture thing matter so much? Well, because creating this culture is driven by a purpose.

The temptation in a Music Director role is to get so immersed in the detail - of song planning, arrangements, band line ups - that we forget to step back and see the big picture: that music and singing in our gatherings are wonderful gifts from God that allow the word of Christ to dwell in us richly (Colossians 3:16). We know that it is through God's word that the Spirit works (Ephesians 6:17) to grow people in Christ-likeness (for example, Galatians 5:22-25).

We want to do everything in our power to help this happen - and I am suggesting that culture is an excellent place to start. So, as Music Directors, *we want to help create a culture that allows the word of Christ to dwell richly among God's people.*

By focusing first on building this kind of culture in our music team, we are offering leadership to the congregation. We are demonstrating what a Word-centred music culture might look like. Musicians are often on the platform in Sunday services – and to congregation members, that placement indicates that musicians are leaders in the church. And we are.

By establishing a purposeful culture, we are also focusing our energies on music and singing as a vehicle for discipleship growth. That will affect what we say between songs, which songs we sing, how we play our instruments, and how we relate to one another in the team.

In the next chapter, we'll consider what this kind of culture might look like.

Greg Cooper

CHAPTER FIVE: What should a music team culture look like?

In the last chapter, I suggested that the unique role of a Music Director is *to help create a culture that allows the word of God to dwell richly among God's people through song*. While the music *culture of the church* is the direct responsibility of the Senior Minister (and the indirect responsibility of the Music Director), the *culture of the music team* is the direct responsibility of the Music Director.

As the music team leads the congregation in song week in, week out, our focused investment in the music team will in turn help lead and encourage the congregation in their singing (and grow church music culture).

So how do we go about intentionally shaping a music team culture? In the last chapter, I suggested 3 steps:

   1. *establishing* the values that you want to see in your team;
   2. *communicating* those values clearly and regularly; and
   3. *practising* (and modeling) those values.

In this chapter, we'll focus on what these 'values' might be.

Values of team culture

If you are leading a church music team, chances are you stepped in and inherited an existing team. Alternatively, you might be part of a church plant where you've helped form the team from the ground up.

In either case – have you ever stepped back and dreamed about what a great team might look like? Sure, we are marred by sin and we will never be perfect. But within the realms of human possibility, what might a great team look like?

Why do some teams in businesses function better than others?

Why do certain sporting teams flourish, while others limp along?

Why are some rock bands a beautifully cohesive unit, while others need separate backstage trailers to avoid conflict?

Obviously there are many factors that lead to these scenarios – it would be naïve to over-simplify. But literature, podcasts, and experience on these topics suggest that establishing clear team values and culture is central to a successful team. It won't fix everything, but it will be giving a team the best chance of being effective.

So what values might help shape an effective church music team? Below are some suggestions. You may agree with some, and disagree with others. That's OK! You may have some values you'd like to add to the list. Importantly, implementing these (or any) values is not a quick task – under God, it will probably take years for them to become part of team culture. You will need to commit for the long haul. In my own experience, I have found it best to try and focus on just a few of these values at any given time. Trying to focus on all of them at once is unlikely to be effective. So, with all those things in mind, let's dive in.

Some suggested values for your team culture:

1. God-centred and Word-soaked

These sound obvious. But in the rush of Sunday rehearsals, and 'getting the job done', it is very easy to forget that our focus must always be God. Our energy is to be directed towards serving him and his people. We musicians love music, gigs, music gear… It's so easy to spend our rehearsal time focused on discussing those things. And of course there's a time for those chats! But we must keep the main thing the main thing.

A great way to do this is to ensure God's word is front and centre in our rehearsals and team meetings. Sure, rehearsals are for rehearsing. They are not Bible studies. But if you're anything like me, you arrive at rehearsals from a busy day, distracted, and thinking about many other things.

So if rehearsal were to commence with a team member opening up God's word and sharing some reflections on a verse or two, wouldn't that be a wonderful service to the team? Wouldn't it help focus us? And then we could commit our distractions and worries and joys to God in prayer, asking for his strength to help us serve. This whole process need only take 5-10 minutes. But in my experience, inviting a team member to serve the team in this way helps centre and spiritually unite the team. It's also a great way of involving team members in a different way.

2. Prayerful and prayer-covered

In addition to praying with the team at rehearsals, are you (as Music Director) praying for the team regularly? For individuals and their spiritual growth and commitment to the team? For the unity of the team as a whole? And does the team know you are praying for them? This is not to boast – quite the opposite. It is to demonstrate your complete dependence on God as you lead. And to show your love for your team.

In the rush of 'getting things done', it is so easy to forget prayer. (I am as guilty of this as anyone.) Prayer sometimes doesn't feel 'productive' – while working through the to-do list does. But we know that it is only through God that anything at all is possible. And that he wants us to cast all our cares on him (1 Peter 5:7).

How about writing 'prayer' at the top of your to do list each day? And praying with another member of staff for the music team?

We can also invite members of our team or members of the church to pray for the music team. This is a great way to share the music team vision with others, and to help them co-own that vision. It's not all up to you! I recall a season of particular difficulty when I was recently serving as a Music Director. The church was going through a season of change, and I was receiving a lot of criticism for changes being made to music. To my surprise, I received a letter from some members of the church assuring me that they were praying for me and the music ministry. What an incredible encouragement and reassurance!

Perhaps there are people at your church you could invite to pray for the music team. After all, if our singing is such a central part of our gatherings, our church members care about it! What a wonderful thing it would be for you and your team to know they are being covered in prayer in this way.

3. The team knows its 'why' and where it is going

In his bestselling book *Start With Why*, Simon Sinek argues that in business, customers are drawn to buy products not because of what the product is, but because of why it exists.

He argues that Apple products, for example, are so popular not because of the precise features of the products. There are many other computers or phones that do the same thing at the same level. Rather, people are drawn to Apple's stated reason for existence – to think differently and challenge the status quo. That is Apple's 'why'.

How do they do this? By making beautifully designed computers and phones.

By extension, employees (for any organisation) who turn up to work each day with a clear sense of 'why' are more satisfied in their jobs.

I firmly believe the same is true of any team. A team that knows its why will, I believe, be more effective – and team members more satisfied in their role.

So in music ministry, we need to be clear in our own minds why we do this ministry and why we believe the team should be doing it as well. Thankfully, we need look no further than God's word. In Colossians 3:16, Paul instructs:

> Let the word of Christ dwell in you richly, teaching and admonishing one another in all wisdom, singing psalms and hymns and spiritual songs, with thankfulness in your hearts to God.

Our singing of 'psalms, hymns and spiritual songs' (which includes our congregational songs) is seeking to allow the word of Christ (the gospel) to dwell richly in the hearts and minds of the congregation. That is our music team's 'why'.

Have we made that clear to our teams? Do they know why they are turning up to church to rehearse and play at church? Do they know why they are sacrificing family time, social commitments and other musical opportunities to rehearse and play? When I started out in music ministry, I did not understand that purpose. I simply knew churches had singing, and we were a band accompanying that singing. I am thankful that others have explained this purpose to me over the years.

By stating this 'why', we are also helping our team to know where it is going. Any team needs a vision or direction in which it is traveling. As Music Director, you might like to set a vision for the team that encourages faithfully using music and song to help the word to dwell in the congregation's hearts and minds every week. The goal is not perfect music but faithful accompaniment and leadership of congregational singing.

Each band can then debrief each week against that (or a similar) benchmark. Did we faithfully lead our congregation in song, allowing God's word to dwell richly among his people? Did the guitar solo perhaps distract from the words? Was the singing leadership clear? Were our arrangements supportive of congregational singing, or were they seeking to draw attention to ourselves?

As you discuss your team's vision with your team members and seek their input and insights, you can continually refine your team's reason for existence, and its vision. Just make sure you communicate these things regularly and clearly to the whole team. Clarity around these issues will help your music team immensely.

4. Clear expectations

Picture a scenario where you are expecting your friend to meet you at 6pm for dinner. 6pm comes and goes… 6.10… 6.20… Your friend turns up at 6.25. You are frustrated – you are sure you had agreed on 6pm.

"Where have you been? I've been waiting for 25 minutes," you boldly declare.

Taken aback, your friend says "But we always meet at 6.30 – in fact, I'm 5 minutes early!"

"Yes, we normally do meet at 6.30, but this week I had to meet earlier, remember? I have to meet someone after this."

"I have no recollection of that whatsoever. I'm sorry if I stuffed up.", says your friend.

Certain you're right, you flick through your text messages to try and prove your point – only to find there is nothing said about it in your text message conversation.

"Hmm. I'm sorry. I don't think I ever communicated that we'd meet at 6. Maybe it was just in my own head."

You can see where this is going. Each person in this scenario had different expectations. The thing about expectations is that we can often assume everyone has the same expectations as us – for an event, timings, a holiday, for how a team will operate, and so on. But two people's expectations are rarely the same. We're individuals, after all.

It's important that we make really clear what is expected of our team members. If this hasn't been done in your team, it's never too late. As Music Director, it is worth you thinking through some possible expectations and then asking your Senior Minister what he expects of the music team. Once you've agreed on some expectations, communicate them to the music team – not just once, but often.

The expectations don't need to be lengthy or elaborate. They just need to capture the core of what your team is to be about.

Some possible expectations might be:

1. Committed to Christ
2. Committed to Church
3. Committed to a small group (or an accountability relationship)
4. Committed to skill development

These expectations were in place when I recently inherited the role of Music Director at a church. The first three focus on our spiritual maturity, while only number four focuses on musical skills. That emphasis was not an accident – in our music teams, spiritual maturity must always take priority over musicianship.

Clear and well-communicated expectations help in anticipating and resolving conflict. By having these expectations clearly laid out, it was like people were signing a contract – if you want to be part of the team, you must agree to these rules. If any team member then struggled in meeting any of the expectations (eg, not coming to church regularly), it was an agreed baseline to open up discussion. I could gently challenge someone on why they hadn't been at church, and whether they were still suited to being on the music team. If I had struggled in my church attendance, any team member could have gently challenged me in the same way.

On the positive side, these expectations will help grow your team in their service of the Lord Jesus. If everyone is regularly attending church and small group and working hard on their musicianship, that will help create a wonderfully encouraging and forward-moving culture in your team.

5. Sense of ownership of the team

I have assumed that the musicians at your church know they are part of a team. But perhaps they don't – perhaps they serve at the gathering they attend and never see musicians from other gatherings.

Having a regular full team meeting is a helpful way to communicate a sense of 'team'. Everyone sees everyone else. Musicians from different bands see each other.

It can even be an excellent first step towards musicians serving at gatherings other than their own. If an evening church band member feels comfortable having met morning church musicians in a social team setting, it makes the idea of serving at morning church much more inviting. We are social creatures – so breaking down barriers to serving outside our comfort zone is important.

One of the biggest frustrations I have observed in Music Directors is a sense that they have to do everything. That no one understands just how much they need to do, and no one chips in to help. Often this is because a sense of 'ownership' of the team hasn't been shared. If you are on staff as a Music Director, or in a volunteer capacity, it is likely that the staff team communicates directly with you about music. The extent to which you keep all that information to yourself or share that information with the team will, in essence, determine where the sense of team ownership lies. If you keep it all to yourself, you'll 'own' the team. But if you share it with the team, the team will own the team.

I believe it is *essential* that the team owns the team.

There is always more work to do than we have time for. The Music Director's role is not to do all the work – rather, it is to empower a team to ensure the work happens. There's a big difference.

HELPING PEOPLE OWN THE TEAM

Here are three ways to help a team own the team:

ONE	TWO	THREE
Meet with your team regularly and communicate the vision, goals, and opportunities for the team.	**Be deeply concerned for the growth and development of each team member.**	**Think carefully about which areas of responsibility you can ask others to be in charge of.**
Invest in your team and show them you love them. Communicate clearly the opportunities for service that exist, and the areas where you personally are struggling in your role – and where their assistance might help this. Invite people to serve.	If you are, you'll want to give them opportunities to serve.	How has God gifted each team member? How can you give them opportunities to use and develop those gifts? Can someone else head up rostering? Or source new songs? Or write the first draft of song selections for the month? Of course, you'll need to give the final approval for things like song selection – but why not invite others to help in the process?

Once those jobs are assigned, **let people do their jobs**. Don't micro-manage. Don't step in when they make a mistake. Let mistakes happen. Help them when patterns of mistakes appear. But let everyone learn. And watch the team grow in maturity.

Watch your language. One of the biggest mistakes I have made when asking people to serve is asking "Can you help me out?". If you're organising something, this is what it feels like people are doing – helping you out by filling a gap in a roster you are overseeing. But it's not at all what is really going on. Instead, we want to invite people to serve – to serve God, the church, and their team. A much better phrase is "I'd like to invite you to serve … would you be willing and interested?". Getting this language right will communicate a sound theology of church and service, rather than a culture of 'getting a job done'. If people are excited by an opportunity to serve, and feel the weight of the need to serve, their sense of team ownership will increase.

Don't be at everything. It's so tempting as Music Director to feel we need to go to every rehearsal and every service. We don't. And we shouldn't. Aside from burning us out, our presence at these things communicates to band leaders that we are micro-managing. It also communicates to our staff team that they can expect us to be at everything. That should not be expected. You might like to drop in to a rehearsal for five minutes towards the end of the rehearsal, to say hi to the team, encourage them, and check everything is on track. But let others own their rehearsals and the music at the gatherings they are serving at.

Be OK to not be frantic. In our culture of 'doing', we can feel like we need to be busy and frantic to justify our worth. This pressure is no less present on a ministry team. It is, of course, a lie. There will be seasons where things are busy. But as Music Director, your constant busyness is not sustainable personally, or beneficial to your team. You are, after all, entrusted with the care and leadership of *people*. By inviting others on the team to take part in certain tasks and leadership roles, it will create time in your schedule. Don't fill that time with more task-centred busyness. Invest in people – meeting with them, reading the Bible with them, praying with and for them. Then maybe take some time to read helpful literature on teams, or ministry. Spend some time setting vision for the team. Write some blog posts that might encourage the team. There are lots of options here. But be OK to not be frantic. If you're like me and love productivity, this will take some getting used to. Know that these new ways of spending your time are a deep and valuable investment in the team.

6. Cared for and defended by their leader

A team needs to know their leader has their best interests at heart, and will defend them.

Church music has always been controversial. Everyone has an opinion. So, if a congregation member approaches you after a service and criticises a singer who was out of tune, or lost their place in a song, resist the urge to go along with their criticism. When people are pushy and opinionated, we can want to please them – they make us feel like their opinion has substantial value.

Fight the urge to people-please. Instead, take a deep breath, count to 5 in your head, and then reply. Thank the person for their feedback and let them know you've heard them. Let them know you are proud of your team and how hard they work, and you are deeply thankful for the way God has gifted them. And then end the conversation. Certainly, if that singer keeps making that mistake, there will be a need to speak with them to see how it can be fixed. But we are all human and we all make mistakes.

Congregation members with strong opinions must not be allowed to derail your team. And you must not criticise a team member behind their back. Defend your team as a demonstration of your love for them.

7. Unity

God's people are to be characterised by unity. The apostle Paul writes in Romans:

> May the God who gives endurance and encouragement give you

> the same attitude of mind toward each other that Christ Jesus had, so that with one mind and one voice you may glorify the God and Father of our Lord Jesus Christ. (Romans 15:5-6)

We are to have the same love for one another that Christ had for us. We are to seek to have one mind and one voice. Why? So that we may bring glory to God.

These are huge goals to be pursuing. But in our consumerist, individualistic culture, we can often downplay just how significant unity is supposed to be in the life of the church, and how pleasing it is to God.

It won't happen on its own – we need to pray for it and work at it.

Music is horribly divisive. It is a sad irony that a gift from God designed to unite us has, in our sinfulness, caused deep division.

That may not be true in your church. I hope it isn't. But my experience suggests that even if not a big problem in churches, division over music will be apparent in small ways. Discontent in the music team over song selection. Non-singing from a congregation member who objects to the lack of hymns being sung. Unspoken frustrations on the staff team about the role of music in church. And so on.

Let us heed the Apostle Paul's call for unity – both within the music team and between the music team and the congregation. It will probably require some tough conversations, and working through areas of conflict. Like in any relationship, it may mean agreeing to disagree on certain things and loving each other anyway. Not because we're just trying to be nice or avoid conflict. But because loving each other brings glory to God.

8. Thinking

Our faith is a thinking faith. Reading the Bible well requires us to think rigourously. So working out how to do biblical music ministry well will require thinking. Encourage that in your team by showing your team that you are constantly thinking through what the Bible calls us to do in our music team. Share your thoughts with them at team meetings, in blog posts, and in conversations after church.

Encourage your team to be thinkers too. Are there people in the team who love reading and writing? Invite them to read some great books on music ministry and share their reflections with the team.

We want a culture of reflection on God's word that then invites careful thought about how we can best serve him and his church every Sunday.

RECOMMENDED READING

You and your team might like to read some of the following books and discuss them:

Ministry

Jeremy S. Begbie, *Resounding Truth*
Harold M. Best, *Unceasing Worship*
Harold M. Best, *Music Through the Eyes of Faith*
D.A. Carson (ed.), *Worship by the Book*
Bob Kauflin, *Worship Matters* **(Read this first!)**
Bob Kauflin, *True Worshippers*
Tim Keller, *Preaching*
Philip Percival, *Then Sings My Soul*
Eugene H. Peterson, *The Contemplative Pastor*
James K.A. Smith, *You Are What You Love*

Creativity & Strategy

Ed Catmull, *Creativity Inc*
Todd Henry, *The Accidental Creative*
Todd Henry, *Louder Than Words*
Simon Sinek, *Start With Why*

9. Honesty

In our music teams, we want a culture where we can be honest with one another. We are leading the congregation in our services – so if our team members are living, behaving, or serving in a way that might hinder godly and effective leadership, we need to be honest about it.

We often find it hard to be honest with one another at church. It can seem rude to be honest. We don't want to offend others or hurt their feelings.

But as I read the gospels, I am struck by the inescapable reality that Jesus was honest with people. He was honest about who he was and how they needed to respond to him. His honesty was an expression of his love.

Certainly, it is possible to say honest things in a way that hurts one another. But if we genuinely seek to demonstrate love through our honesty, we will go a long way towards avoiding this.

When thinking about honesty, it's helpful to think about 2 things:
- the *content* of what needs to be said;
- the manner in which it is said.

In considering a matter that needs honest discussion, I would recommend first thinking carefully about the *content* of what needs to be said. Maybe write the issues down in a notepad, or discuss them with a trusted colleague.

- Did a songleader's conduct at a party on Saturday night raise questions about their spiritual maturity, and undermine their leadership?
- Did your drummer overplay in the service and appear to be drawing attention to himself?
- Is the flute player only coming to church when rostered on for music, and not really prioritising their walk with Jesus above their music ministry?

In any of these scenarios, discern what the real issue is. Think carefully and pray about how that issue might be addressed.

Then think and pray about the *manner* in which you will address that issue with the person. Do not talk about the relevant person and issue behind their back. It can feel much easier to complain about someone to others, rather than actually addressing the person. But in Matthew 18:15-16 Jesus says that if a brother (or sister) sins against us, we are to address that person first. If they will not listen, then – and only then – involve others in conversation with the person. You may need to seek the wisdom of a trusted colleague about how to approach the issue with the person. That is purposeful and specific third party involvement. But what is important is that third parties don't become involved unnecessarily.

A face to face conversation is always best. Avoid text messages, emails and even phone calls. Feedback is difficult to hear – so facial expressions and body language are essential ingredients in helping feedback to be delivered (and heard) appropriately.

Always seek to encourage the person in their ministry too. Ideally we want the first and last words of the feedback conversation to be encouraging words. That way the difficult words of feedback are heard in a context of encouragement, and the person leaves the conversation feeling challenged but excited about continuing to serve. These kinds of conversations are never easy, but will become more natural in time.

Seek to create a culture in your team where feedback is seen as additive, not competitive – that is, where honest conversations are *adding* to the team's effectiveness, rather than creating competition (or conflict) between people. Being a leader who willingly accepts feedback yourself will help this. Giving regular, honest feedback to others will also help. Also, encourage team members to give feedback to each other – so it's not just about the music director giving feedback. Feedback will become a natural part of team discussions, rather than an 'event' to be feared.

When should we give feedback? I would suggest giving feedback primarily when patterns of behaviour are observed. We all have off-days when we sing out of tune, miss entries, or start songs in the wrong time signature. Try not to give team members constructive feedback at each of those moments. They'll know they messed up. But if things like this are happening in a pattern, then it may need to be brought to the person's attention. Maybe they are always late to rehearsal, or always play too loud. These kinds of patterns need addressing.

The exception to waiting for patterns before giving feedback is when matters of spiritual maturity and Christian behaviour are involved. These matters need to be addressed as they occur. This is not just for the sake of the team, but as an expression of love towards the relevant person, for the sake of their relationship with God.

If an issue arises at a Sunday service, it is often best to wait a day or two before giving feedback. This allows some distance and objectivity from the events. Some matters may need urgent discussion as they occur. But generally, it is best to pick a conversation time when you and the person you are speaking with are both relaxed and not busy with serving.

10. Pursues skilfulness in the name of love

I've suggested above that spiritual maturity is always more important than musical skill level. It is.

But skill is still a consideration. Psalm 33:3 says:

> "Sing to him a new song;'
> play skilfully, and shout for joy."

I think of skill as the development of God-given gifts. To steward those gifts well, it is our responsibility to work at them. Practice, learn, take lessons, play lots – whatever it takes. Enjoy the gifts God has given you and your team members! But also grow in skill so those skills can be used for the encouragement of God's people through song.

I believe a team should be working together at skill development, and encouraging each other when they see improvements. It's a beautiful thing to witness such conversations.

As Music Director, you can help your musicians grow in their skills. Run training sessions to help them think through how to play well in a band. Invite guest speakers who can help your team in certain areas. Encourage your team members to consider taking lessons. And –

importantly – roster your bands in a way that allows team members to play with the same musicians regularly. Just like in a sporting team, this week-in-week-out consistency will help everyone grow in ensemble skills.

I suggested above that being 'Committed to skill development' is a good expectation to have of your team. I believe it really is. We're not asking anyone to be perfect at their instrument – but it is good and right to want to grow and move forward and steward well the gifts God has given us!

11. Disciple-making

Seeking to build disciple-making into our music team culture starts by zooming out, and getting back to basics about why the music team exists at all. The team exists to serve and honour God by serving his people – the church. The team exists to help strengthen and grow God's church.

As the Apostle Paul says to the church in Corinth, "Everything must be done so that the church may be built up." (1 Corinthians 14:26b). We also know that our churches exist to carry out Jesus' command that we "make disciples of all nations… teaching them to obey everything I have commanded you." (Matthew 28:19-20). We don't do this alone. We – the church – are "the temple of the living God", and God promises to be with us and amongst us (2 Corinthians 6:16).

What, then, does disciple-making look like? Sarie King of Effective Ministry helpfully defines disciple-making as "an intentional, relational, Christ-oriented activity, exercised by every believer, to use every opportunity in encouraging and teaching others to know, grow, and faithfully follow Jesus." As the Effective Ministry website states, "If we're to achieve and renew gospel growth, then deliberately and intentionally growing disciple-making disciples must begin to form the very DNA of each and every church, and each and every believer." (www.effectiveministry.org/about)

Are our team members seeking to build one another up in Christ? Are our teams looking outwards to include others into the church – and the team?

Chapter Five: What should a music team culture look like?

Some small steps in this direction might include:
- Asking each team member to look out for another team member in their walk with Christ. They might like to read the Bible together, pray together, or share aspects of their lives together. Even the smallest intentional conversation about our walk with Jesus can bear great fruit.
- Asking each team member to be intentional about finding other (possibly younger) members of the church they can look to train up and welcome in to the music team. A guitarist might like to train up younger guitarist, for example. This requires a long-term investment – it takes time to train others. But it is an act of service towards the team, and the church – after all, you may leave the church or step aside from music ministry in the future. It is important to be thinking about the future of the team.
- Challenging each team member to share the gospel with their friends and family. Keep this on the radar by praying about it as a team and inviting team members to share about how their relationships with non-believers are progressing. When team members bring their non-Christian friends to church, other music team members can then be the first to welcome the guest.

Although these steps seem separate to the making of music, they are in fact integral to the making of music *for the church*. Church music is about more than the music – it's about music as a means to strengthen and encourage the church for the glory of God. Thinking intentionally about disciple-making as we make music will help to keep this purpose front and centre.

12. Team of teams

You may be the Music Director (or music co-ordinator or leader) but that doesn't mean you have to do all the leading. In fact, you shouldn't be doing all the leading. You are, in fact, a leader of leaders. You are helping leaders within your team to carry out their roles.

A great way to carry this out in practice is to think of the music team as a team of smaller teams. The smaller teams might be bands, prayer teams, social event teams, or sound teams. Each of these teams will need a leader.

You might also invite a team member from each Sunday service to lead music at that service – they could think critically about the effectiveness of music at that service, care for the musicians there, and source new songs. And then these leaders can report back to you.

Your job is to care for and lead those leaders.

This not only helps things get done – it also means that you can strategically invest in the lives of the leaders, and influence the work of the music team through your investment in those leaders. Rather than you being involved in every little detail, you are like an umbrella over those leaders – caring for them, praying for them, and challenging them.

13. Creative

As creatures of the Creator – made in his image – we have the gift of being able to create. Music by its very nature is creative. After all, it doesn't just exist – it gets created.

If we embrace with gratitude the gift of creativity, the possibilities of the music we can make are limitless. But this starting point of gratitude is crucial.

As Jeremy S. Begbie writes,

> "the most basic response of the Christian toward music will be *gratitude*. This does not mean giving unqualified thanks for every bit of music we hear, but it will mean being thankful for the very possibility of music. It will mean regularly allowing a piece of music to stop us in our tracks and make us grateful *that there is* a world where music can occur, *that there is* a reality we call 'matter' that oscillates and resonates, *that there is* sound, *that there is* rhythm built into the fabric of the world, *that there is* the miracle of the human body, which can receive and process sequences of tones. For from all this and through all this, the marvel of music is born. None of it *had* to come into being. But

it has, for the glory of God and for our flourishing. Gaining a Christian mind on music means learning the glad habit of thanksgiving." (*Resounding Truth*, p 213)

Perhaps our churches like music to sound a certain way – and that can feel constraining to creativity. I would suggest that it is completely right that our leaders (usually our Senior Minister) ask for our music to sound a certain way in order that we serve and build up our congregations. That is part of us submitting to the leader of our church. What's more, all art is created within constraints – whether they relate to finances, personnel, or time. From there, the very process of making music within those constraints is itself a wonderful opportunity for creativity.

As we seek to allow the word of Christ to dwell richly in the hearts of the congregation, how can we use our instruments and voices in beautiful ways?

Are there ways we can slightly vary an arrangement to help people notice words more?

If we have played one song the same way for ten years, can we adjust the instrumentation, or the feel, so certain words are accentuated? I was struck by a new version of *When I Survey* at my own church recently. It was much slower than I'd ever sung it before – and as a result, I noticed nuances in the words I had simply overlooked before. You may like to discuss this with your Senior Minister, and see which aspects of the music can be adjusted from week to week.

It will always be a fine balance between pushing creative boundaries, and 'serving the song' so that its true character and lyrics are left imprinted on the hearts and minds of the congregation. But it is the very pursuit of that fine balance that will create great music.

Some members of your team may be gifted in identifying opportunities for creativity. Why not invite them to form a team to think these matters through? Why not create a songwriting team? Why not have bands that record their own original songs? The possibilities are endless.

In the process of carrying out our role as church musicians week to week, let's remember the gift that music is and enjoy its essence as a creative art.

14. Fun!

Last, but certainly not least! Do you enjoy leading your team? Do you enjoy playing music with them? Let them know! If you have fun, so will they. And encourage them to enjoy themselves too. Let's be honest – music is a lot of fun. Yes, we have lots of things to think through as we serve. But music is a gift to be enjoyed!

A friend of mine takes lollies for band members to every rehearsal – it keeps it fun. You'll have your own ways of making it fun. As you do, thank God for the absolute joy it is to be in a team with the servants he has placed you amongst. And as you serve him and his people, smile – and encourage your team to do the same. People notice smiles – and they communicate an uncontainable joy bursting from the heart. You will be showing your congregation what a joy it is to be leading them in the glorious gift of song.

These are just a few ideas that might help us build a music team culture. There's lots to think about – so it's best to just focus on one or two of these ideas at a time. And the list we've discussed is not exhaustive! You might like to take some time now to write down some of your own ideas for your team.

What would a faithful and loving music team look like at your church? That is a question we can continually ask ourselves. We never 'arrive' - it is a journey of growth as a team.

My prayer is that God will equip you, strengthen you, and grant you abundant joy as you lead your team in this challenging, but important and exciting, ministry of God's word.

Steve Crain

CHAPTER SIX: Is music ministry really about music?
Finding your part in the growth of the Body of Christ

I've been playing guitar in church since I was 14, and from the very first time I played I think there's been a roster to tell me and others when to serve. When I started to run a music ministry, of course I made sure there was a roster. After a while at doing this, I began to be employed by my church to do music ministry, and I got to wondering what was really driving peoples' service? There were things about the music at my church that I wanted to see improve, but in all honesty, that darn roster seemed to be the thing that got people motivated! Surely, I thought, there has to be more to doing this well that being driven by a *roster!*

Driven by the gospel

Of course there is so much more that drives our music ministries, and it all comes back to the Good News, the Gospel, that lets us know who God is, who we are, how humanity has wrecked the relationship between us and God, and how God, in Jesus, has finally made a way back into right relationship with God possible. That relationship is one where we are adopted by God to be his children. We become disciples of our Saviour Jesus, following in his footsteps as a servant, learning how to live from him, motivated by the grace that has been shown to us. At the cross we see we both that our sin is so serious that Jesus had to die, but also that his love for us is so great that he chose to do that. Our pride is humbled as we realize we are utterly unable to save ourselves, and our fears taken away as we see the enormity of his love for us in choosing to pay the penalty for our sin.

As we read the bible we further come to understand that we are not only saved from our sin, but we have been given a new life, a new family, and an intimate relationship with our Father in heaven.

King David writes in Psalm 139:4, "Before a word is on my tongue you, Lord, know it completely," and also later in verse 13 he writes that, "For you created my inmost being; you knit me together in my mother's womb." Further, in verse 16 we learn that, "All the days ordained for me were written in your book before one of them came to be". This is a picture of our creator who knows us intimately as individuals.

Not only that, but from Ephesians 2:10 we learn that, "we are God's handiwork, created in Christ Jesus to do good works, which God prepared in advance for us to do."

Not only have we been created to do good works, but we have been given God's Spirit so that we are equipped by him for these works of service that he has prepared for us to do. He has a plan for us of good works for us to do and he creates and equips us for these good works (even the good works of writing rosters!)

So in the rest of this chapter we will look at the four key passages in the New Testament that will shape our view of spiritual gifts and how they in turn help shape our music ministry. These key passages are: 1 Corinthians 12, Romans 12, 1 Peter 4, and Ephesians 4. Through these passages we will form a picture of the key attitude that goes with spiritual gifts, that of being a Faithful Steward. We will also see how how gift stewardship fits into the bigger picture of how the body of Christ grows.

But first, what is a spiritual gift?

Playing guitar is a spiritual gift

Now, there are more than twenty gifts listed in the New Testament, so the natural first question is, "Is that all of them?" There are three things to note:

1. All the lists of gifts are different,

2. No one gift appears on every list, and

3. No one list contains all of the gifts mentioned.

This leads us to conclude that these lists are not an exhaustive catalogue of all the gifts, but instead in these lists Paul is setting out to explain how the gifts interact in the Body of Christ, and how we are to use and not misuse these gifts. Paul isn't trying to write a definitive catalogue of Spiritual Gifts.

So then, what's a good definition of a Spiritual Gift if it's not just those listed in the New Testament?

Graham Cole in his book on the Spirit *"He Who Gives Life"* quotes Boyd Hunt for this definition:

> "Spiritual Gifts are God **empowering** His people **through** the Holy Spirit **for** kingdom life and service, **enabling** them in attitude and action to **live and minister** in a manner which **glorifies** Christ."

That's a lot to take in though, so I've developed another definition that tries to encompass this definition…. but that hurts my head less…

Steve's Definition:

"Doin' the best you can, with what you've got, for Jesus".

I hope that gives you some easy handles to get a grip on this stuff.

OK then Steve, so spiritual gifts are any of the listed gifts in these passages, or doing anything else really that promotes Jesus, right?

Yep, that's right. And so playing an instrument, singing, doing sound, lugging gear, and even making the band a great coffee before the early Sunday morning rehearsal can be stewarding your spiritual gift. Pretty exciting, huh?!

But there are also a few more layers to it. So let's start with our first key spiritual gift passage.

1 Corinthians 12 and the attitude of service

The main image for the church and spiritual gifts that Paul uses (it's in the three passages that he writes) is that of the church being the "Body of Christ". By understanding the image and the logic of the metaphor we can see there are certain facts about spiritual gifts that shape the attitudes we are to have towards these gifts.

> There are different kinds of gifts, but the same Spirit distributes them. *⁵ There are different kinds of service, but the same Lord. ⁶ There are different kinds of working, but in all of them and in everyone it is the same God at work.*
>
> *⁷ Now to each one the manifestation of the Spirit is given for the common good. ⁸ To one there is given through the Spirit a message of wisdom, to another a message of knowledge by means of the same Spirit, ⁹ to another faith by the same Spirit, to another gifts of healing by that one Spirit, ¹⁰ to another miraculous powers, to another prophecy, to another distinguishing between spirits, to another speaking in different kinds of tongues, and to still another the interpretation of tongues. ¹¹ All these are the work of one and the same Spirit, and he distributes them to each one, just as he determines.* (1 Corinthians 12:4-11)

In 1 Cor 12:7 we read, "Now to each is given the manifestation of the Spirit for the common good."

Gifts are given for the common good, not for our own self esteem, and certainly are not for us to be proud about. Unlike, say, a birthday gift, the primary reason for the gift being given is not for the pleasure or benefit of the gift receiver, but for everyone else in the Body of Christ.

This should produce an attitude of **service** in us.

> All these are the work of one and the same Spirit, and he distributes them to each one, just as he determines ...
>
> And God has placed in the church first of all apostles, second prophets, third teachers, then miracles, then gifts of healing, of helping, of guidance, and of different kinds of tongues. ²⁹ *Are all apostles? Are all prophets? Are all teachers? Do all work miracles? ³⁰ Do all have gifts of healing? Do all speak in tongues? Do all interpret? ³¹ Now eagerly desire the greater gifts.* (1 Corinthians 12:11, 28-30)

Gifts are given by the Spirit, as *he* decides. Not us – we don't get to have a say in what gift we are given, nor do we get a chance to complain because the gift or gifts I have are not the one(s) I would like. We don't get to be grumpy if we don't get to do what we'd like to do! There is no room for envy or jealousy.

Romans 12 and the attitude of humility

> For by the grace given me I say to every one of you: Do not think of yourself more highly than you ought, but rather think of yourself with sober judgment, in accordance with the faith God has distributed to each of you. *4 For just as each of us has one body with many members, and these members do not all have the same function, 5 so in Christ we, though many, form one body, and each member belongs to all the others. 6 We have different gifts, according to the grace given to each of us. If your gift is prophesying, then prophesy in accordance with your faith; 7 if it is serving, then serve; if it is teaching, then teach; 8 if it is to encourage, then give encouragement; if it is giving, then give generously; if it is to lead, do it diligently; if it is to show mercy, do it cheerfully.* (Romans 12:3-8)

"Do not think of yourself more highly than you ought, but rather think of yourself with sober judgment." Don't think too highly or too lowly of yourself. No gift works alone, but the whole body works together, so accurately assessing what your contribution needs to be is very important. The rest of that Romans passage goes on to urge the Romans to find *their* gift, and get on with stewarding that gift – doing the best they can with what they've got. They aren't to compare their gifts, or wish they had someone else's gift – just to get on with stewarding their own gift.

This is different to the culture we live in, right? The world says we are to find self worth and rank ourselves against others based on how well we do things, and we are to compete to see who can be the best, and to earn the most. We are to be self promoters to get ahead. *But not so for us, as we follow Jesus.* We are to be other person centred, and to be servant hearted, looking first to the needs of others. In my area of work beyond Barneys (where I work as the part time Music Minister), I work as a freelance guitarist, and out there in music-land this competitive attitude rules, with people's self worth and value often being based on their musical skills, and those with lesser skill levels often being looked down on, less accepted or included, or even excluded.

Our attitude is to be radically different in the attitude we bring to the use of our gifts.

One way to do this is to "hold your gift loosely"

By this I mean certainly do hold your gift – care for it, nurture and develop it, use it and know all you can about it. But don't hold on to it so tightly that changing the way if gets used threatens you. Those who hold their gift loosely will be best able to hear constructive criticism because their gift isn't their source of self worth, and they want to learn how to grow their gift and achieve the potential that God has built into them. (By the way, I learnt this very helpful attitude and phrase from Rory Noland's book *The Heart of The Artist*. It's well worth a read!)

1 Peter 4 and the attitude of faithfulness

Another crucial attitude to bring to the use of gifts is outlined in our third passage, 1 Peter 4. In verse 10 we read:

> Each of you should use whatever gift you have received to serve others, as faithful stewards of God's grace in its various forms.
> [11] *If anyone speaks, they should do so as one who speaks the very words of God. If anyone serves, they should do so with the strength God provides, so that in all things God may be praised through Jesus Christ. To him be the glory and the power for ever and ever. Amen.* (1 Peter 4:10-11)

"Each of you should use whatever gift you have received to serve others, as faithful stewards of God's grace in its various forms." Clearly we are to have the attitude of a faithful servant. Let's look at the words of Jesus in Matthew 25 to better understand what it means to be a faithful steward.

This parable comes in a series in Matthew 25 about Judgement day and the End times. Jesus starts off by saying "It will be like..." When Jesus tells you that this is what something will be like it's well worth paying attention!

The parable is about three servants – how they respond to what has been entrusted to them. This is not just a parable about money, but about all that has been entrusted to us, including our Spiritual Gifts.

In the parable, the Master represents God, and the servants represent us, his servants. The first two servants get straight to work stewarding what has been entrusted to them, and from the parable it's very clear that what they have been given is not theirs – it's the Master's.

So here is our first point of application – how are you going with your gift stewardship? What do you think the Master would say to you if he was here right now, and what would he think of your current gift stewardship?

Returning to the passage, we note also the first two servants aren't at all envious of each other for what they have been, or have not been given. They don't compare, and they don't compete. They are expected to do the best they can with what they have been given and they get on with doing that.

Note too that they receive equal praise when the Master returns. The same reward is given to both the first two servants, despite one producing 2½ times the actual return of the other. The Master says to both, "Well done good and faithful servant! You have been faithful with a few things; I will put you in charge of many things. Come and share your master's happiness!"

However, when we come to the third servant, things end badly for him. The Master says he is wicked and lazy for burying what has been entrusted to him. The servant even claims to be afraid of the Master, but that isn't a legitimate excuse. He should have stewarded what was entrusted to him.

Reader, if you've been burying what has been entrusted to you, please go dig it up and start using it! Sorry to be pointed, but it's gotta be better to hear it from me than to one day hear it from the Master!

We all have a responsibility to steward the gifts that have been entrusted to us.

Ephesians 4 and the goal of gift stewardship

Our fourth passage is Ephesians 4, and this contains God's Methodology for how Gift Stewardship works – how it matures the individual who stewards their gift and in turn the maturity of the entire Body of Christ.

> So Christ himself gave the apostles, the prophets, the evangelists, the pastors and teachers, [12] *to equip his people for works of service, so that the body of Christ may be built up* [13] *until we all reach unity in the faith and in the knowledge of the Son of God and become mature, attaining to the whole measure of the fullness of Christ.*
>
> [14] *Then we will no longer be infants, tossed back and forth by the waves, and blown here and there by every wind of teaching and by the cunning and craftiness of people in their deceitful scheming.*
>
> [15] *Instead, speaking the truth in love, we will grow to become in every respect the mature body of him who is the head, that is, Christ.* [16] *From him the whole body, joined and held together by every supporting ligament, grows and builds itself up in love, as each part does its work.*
> (Ephesians 4:11-16)

There are three sections to this Ephesians passage.
- Section 1: verses 11-13
- Section 2: verse 14
- Section 3: verses 15-16

Section 1 shows how five specific gifts (Apostles, Prophets, Evangelists, Pastors and Teachers) are given to equip the rest of the body of Christ for works of service. Stewarding of these gifts enables the clear understanding of giftings and enables good works to occur.

Section 2 shows what happens if these five gifts are not stewarded – the body remains as an infant, "tossed back and forth by the waves, and blown here and there by every wind of teaching and by the cunning and craftiness of people in their deceitful scheming".

Section 3 works like the second stage of the first section. As each part does its work, the body grows as each gift is stewarded and each part of the body ministers to others as is needed. And all of this works as the truth is spoken in love. The truth which is being spoken is not just any old truth, but the good news of Jesus.[7] But truth conversations don't end once we become a Christian – discipleship means continually bringing the gospel to bear on each other's lives. I'm convinced that a crucial chunk of those gospel conversations needs to be made up of honest and open communication about how we're going with our gift stewardship.

All gifts are needed to grow the church towards maturity. Your gift really matters! Don't fall into the error of thinking that spiritual growth comes just from hearing the Word taught (though of course this is wonderful and necessary). The text doesn't say that! It says that grow occurs as "each part does its work". The five "primary" giftings set up the other gifts. So, if you want to grow, then steward your spiritual gift! If you want your church and the Kingdom as a whole to grow, then steward your spiritual gift!

Summary

1. Spiritual Gifts are anything you can do to serve Jesus and his church in an other person centred way. "Do the best you can with what you've got, for Jesus".
2. Our attitude is to be that of a Faithful Steward. Faithful stewardship is our responsibility. Matthew 25 tells us that we will be called to account for what we have done with what has been entrusted to us.
3. Ephesians 4 shows us God's Methodology for growing the Church – speaking the Truth in love about our Gift Stewardship.

---

[7] The same words is used in Gal 4:16; see Peter T O'Brien, **The Letter to the Ephesians**, 311.

But, it's not ALL about responsibility.

Do you remember where we started?

Psalm 130 tells us we are fully know by God and that we are part of His plan. Ephesians 2 tells us that we have been created for doing good works, and that in fact God has even prepared the in advance for us to do!

And because he has planned these good works for us to do, we don't need to try to be motivated in our serving by simply having our name come up on a roster. It's not just that we should all chip in a bit and take our turn on a roster. No – these are acts of service that have been planned by God for millennia! It's what you have been put on the planet to do! You, and your unique contribution through your gift has been planned for the moment you have the opportunity to serve by none less that God himself! How inspiring is that!?!

But can I share one more thing with you? Despite the hugely inspiring fact that God himself has planned each chance you have to serve with your gift, the bad news is…you aren't going to be able to do it right. We all find ways to mess up being a servant – we get envious of others' gifts, or the attention or acclaim they get, or we end up playing or singing in a way that wants at least some of the glory to come our way rather than it all going to Jesus, or we feel like the "one bag of gold" we have been entrusted with is too small and we feel it's too hard to steward, too small to steward, or feel it's too small to base our self worth on (which of course we shouldn't be basing it on anyway!).

Friends, we all fall so far short of being faithful stewards! But what we are called to do is to look to the one who is your perfect and faithful steward, the one who,

> being in very nature God,
> *did not consider equality with God something to be used to his own advantage;*
> [7] rather, he made himself nothing
> *by taking the very nature of a servant,*
> *being made in human likeness.*

> [8] And being found in appearance as a man,
> *he humbled himself*
> *by becoming obedient to death—*
> *even death on a cross!* (Philippians 2:6-8)

When you face challenges in your gift stewardship — look to him! See Jesus, who is worthy of all praise, humbling himself to wash your feet, not repaying your insults with insult, nor repaying your cool distance with anything but warm embrace, nor taking offence at your offences but being slow to anger and abounding in mercy. See him laying down his life for you, taking on the punishment that your sin deserves. Faithful stewardship does not come from trying harder, but instead from coming to the cross and being captivated again by the humble servant who "saved a wretch like me".

It is an astounding privilege to have anything at all that I might be able to contribute to God's work in the world. But that he has designed a method for my unique abilities and personality to work together as part of his design is amazing! His holiness and love are shown at the cross, and my fears and pride are overcome, replaced by courage and humility. What a joy to serve him who gave his all for me! How marvellous, how wonderful, is my Saviour's love for me!

TAKING FEEDBACK

Andy Judd

Everybody has their own taste in music, which is great – the world would be a boring place if we all listened to the same playlists. But what makes music ministry hard is that often people will (consciously or unconsciously) elevate their preferred style of music to something more. When taste becomes theological you know you're in trouble. *'It's not just that I prefer classical music; it's the how worship should be.'* Part of the job of Music Director is to take criticism and feedback well. Here are some tips:

1. Look at the person. Smile at them. However annoying you may find them, remember that you were far worse and yet God loved you (Romans 5:8). Remember they are precious to God.

2. Every time someone gives feedback is an opportunity for growth, on both sides. As a minister, your goal should be to help them to grow in their Christian understanding and maturity (as well as, obviously, taking on board observations which might help you improve your own ministry). This means that even completely misguided feedback is an opportunity to think together about music ministry.

3. Never read anonymous feedback. It's not worth the paper it's written on.

4. Emails are good for sharing information, but they are terrible for communication. If it is an emotional issue try (if at all possible) to speak in person or over the phone.

5. When someone gives you feedback, respond first with questions rather than statements. Usually feedback comes in highly vague global statements ('it's too much of a performance!'), and it's not always clear what they mean. If you feel like you are banging your head against the wall, don't assume they are an idiot. Instead, try to get to the root of the disagreement by helping them make explicit the assumptions which are behind their perspective. What data are they working from? How have their interpreted that data? What

philosophy is guiding them? What positive desires do they feel are under threat?

6. Get in first – before the feedback strikes. People might not realise what you're trying to do, for instance, by putting a particular song in the set list. When Steve Crain sends out the songs for the week he gives a detailed explanation for why he has chosen each song. This trains people to think about how the themes of each song fit with the message of the service, rather than just complaining that their favourite song was not included.

7. Seek out the feedback you need. It's easy to have your radar filled with an unrepresentative sample of opinions. Work out who you should be listening to, and what questions you want them to answer.

8. The way feedback is given or received often has more to do with who is in the conversation rather than what they are talking about. Have a think about the person giving you feedback. How are they different from you? Why are they telling you? How do they see your respective roles? Is the feedback directly about you or is it really about someone else?

9. Finally, be aware of your own personality when it comes to feedback. Some of us communicate directly and take highly negative comments in our stride – these people may need to be more sensitive to feedback or they'll miss it! But, in contrast, I know that I have a huge amount of my identity caught up in my music – when I bare my soul in music, and someone says my soul isn't very good, it stings. I need to be careful not to take negative feedback as a threat to my identity, which I know is ultimately secure in Christ who loves me despite my performance. I also need to be aware that there are certain times when I am particularly vulnerable to negative feedback, and I know that I will take more time to bounce back to my baseline emotional level afterwards.

Further reading: *Thanks for the Feedback* by Douglas Stone and Sheila Heen (2014).

Mark Peterson

CHAPTER SEVEN: Team building

I think I need a holiday. A really good one. My music team is not specifically asking me to have one, but I think it will be good for them too. As I write, I have eight weeks of long service leave planned … my family and I will be 1600 kilometres away from our home in Adelaide and just 150 metres from the beach. That should be perfect. I'm praying for a great eight weeks!

I am sure there will be the benefits of refreshment. Perhaps I should start thinking about what novels I'll read. For the first couple of weeks, I'll need a siesta (or two) every day just to be able to stay upright. It's been a busy decade of leading music ministry in my church at Holy Trinity Adelaide.

However, refreshment is only one of the reasons that I think this holiday will be good. The other reason is that sometimes you need to get out of the way to enable your leaders to lead.

You see, the long service leave is a bit of a test. I want the leaders in my music ministry to share responsibility with me. For that eight week period that I am not around, the leaders will need to own what happens with the music in our gatherings. Either that, or problems will occur, and I am not sure who will address them.

There will be a list of things that they will need to do… there always is. But beyond the question of tasks, will they feel that they need to work together to bring about the best outcomes for our gatherings? Will they feel a sense of personal responsibility for how music sounds, and for whether the people in our gatherings are uplifted, taught and reminded by the songs? Will they care deeply for the people in their teams and for God receiving honour and glory by the way things run?

I am not asking for anything different from an ordinary Sunday when the Music Director is present. There is no point having goals for people, gatherings or sounds unless my team has similar goals. We all need to share the goals on our shoulders together, or we are all going to get frustrated and not do as much good as we otherwise could.

So in fact, my time away is not a test of my leaders. It is a test of my own leadership. If I have not, in the lead up to my time away, cultivated shared hopes and aspirations for our music ministry, then it is unlikely that they will be demonstrated when I am not around.

Building a team by building leaders

The most important way to build your music team is to build your team of leaders well. Who are the people around you who have ideas and initiative, who seem to want to make the music better? Who are the ones who attract the respect of others, who have skills with managing people and processes? Who are the members of your team who are a good example to others?

1. Preparing to empower (clarifying leadership structure)

You may feel that you can already think of people in your wider team who could be leaders. That is excellent. Every year I need to be nudged to go through my lists of names and think about leadership possibilities.

But I encourage you to pause before you jump. Have you considered what leadership roles would bring about the greatest benefit in your context? Who would your leaders actually lead?

This raises the vital question of leadership structure, and you really need to think it through carefully before you go too far into setting people up with expectations. In an organisational context, this is the "organisational chart". Over the years, management experts have exerted much time and energy into identifying the best accountability structures for organisations. They have often tried to move away from the traditional hierarchical models that have overtones of an authoritarian approach.

The principle in this is: Every role has some responsibility attached to it, and a person (or group) to whom a person in that role is accountable for fulfilling that responsibility. When that role and responsibility involves other peoples' contribution, it is leadership.[8]

I have often found in churches I have visited that there is a great reluctance to formalize leadership in music teams. Perhaps we see creative people as needing space away from organizational structures so that they can achieve to the best of their ability.

In my experience, the opposite is often the case. Although creative people are sometimes reluctant to be structured, it tends to bring better results when our roles are clarified. The classic example is a rehearsal without a leader, or with a leader who does not see him- or herself as needing to make decisions. This creates two possible negative outcomes: either there is a seemingly endless discussion of options leading to staggered progress, or someone else who is not the leader assumes control.

When people know what their role is, they are much more likely to be fruitful in their role. When roles continue to change, progress is difficult, both for the team as a whole and for individuals. So think this through carefully before you begin recruiting.

Here are three possible models of how to structure leadership:

- **Informal but influential** You could form a small group of leaders selected because of their experience and enthusiasm for music ministry. You could meet with them periodically to review aspects of how music is going and to consider initiatives and changes that you could roll out according to a plan and schedule. This model might work well if your music team is small or medium sized, where team members are rostered on a week-by-week needs basis.

---

8 In the business literature, a distinction is often made between *leadership*, which is about setting vision, mission and reinforcing an appropriate culture, and *management*, which is about managing people and processes (e.g. see John P. Kotter, *Leading Change*). In the church, we often use the term *leader* to describe what may align better with the secular term *manager*.

- **A range of gifts mobilised** You could try to identify particular tasks that, due to your own limited time, energy or skills, are not being done. For example, a team full of superbly gifted creative musicians might benefit from the administrative, IT/web, project management or even pastoral gifts of others. Recruit people to responsibilities that will enable you to focus your own energies better, using your skills most appropriately.
- **Formal accountability structure** You might establish a high level of clarity in your music system, with specific roles. For example, each distinct band might have a leader responsible for most of the activities of the band, including song selection, backfilling unavailabilities, coordinating and running rehearsals, liaising with wider ministry team. You could term these leaders Band Leaders, Band Coordinators, Song Leaders, or Interns, depending on their specific responsibilities. This sort of structure might suit a large church with music teams that spread over more than one gathering.

When I started my role in 2005, I began with the "informal but influential" model of leaders. I had only just begun, but I knew I could not get far without getting key people onside reasonably quickly. I asked for input from some of my staff colleagues and from the previous Music Director, and pulled together a team who would meet about six times per year. It was called the Music Round Table, and I think the name of the group helped to communicate that this was a team of equals, where every member was able to contribute.

At the time, our church had five regular Sunday gatherings. Four of the seven members of the Music Round Table represented their own gathering (one person represented two very similarly styled gatherings). Two other members of the group had roles focused on music ministry "development". One of these had an internal focus, thinking about developing our processes and some support technologies. The other had an external focus, thinking about how to use music as an outreach. As the seventh member of the team, I was the chair.

This worked well for several years. We identified training needs and ran simple training events to meet some of these needs. We ran some evangelistic music evenings with mixed success. We spent considerable time talking and thinking about the role of music in church, formulating statements of vision and mission. We then hosted a series of events that enabled us to model the use of music slightly differently from how it was seen and understood in our Sunday gatherings. We enabled people to experience music differently and reflect on it.

In the end, several things happened at once and we changed the structure. First, our church was about to plant two new churches simultaneously, meaning that our network of churches would go from three to five centres overnight. We needed to start thinking Trinity Network instead of just Trinity City.

Second, I was feeling that the area I really wanted to develop my leaders in was the hands-on running of music week by week, rather than simply in the discussion of principles and vision for the future. This came from thinking through the need to be equipping people not only to lead music ministry in our own church, but also to develop skills that would be transportable to other churches, should their situations change and they move elsewhere.

So I moved more deliberately to the "formal accountability structure" approach, which is how we are structured presently. Prior to this, there were some formal roles. Band Coordinators looked after the organizing side of each band, and Music Leaders would run rehearsals (or if I were running the rehearsals, I would give them opportunities to shape the sound of the music).

However, it wasn't quite working the way I had hoped. By separating administration out from musical decisions, I had set up a system in which no-one was really taking responsibility. One person sent emails and text messages, another ran rehearsals, but neither of them really felt that they had been given the opportunity to "own" a band and develop it.

I should stress that this was a problem with the structure I had set up, rather than the fault of any of the highly committed individuals. The leadership I was expecting people to adopt was fractured. The Music

Leaders were not learning about pulling the band together, and the Band Coordinators were not learning about making musical decisions. To add to this, I had six of my most experienced music leaders heavily committed to the Music Round Table, which was effectively distracting them from developing bands.

I now wanted to develop a crop of musical leaders who would own all the details of music ministry in the band for which they were rostered, rather than just partial ownership of some of the details of the music ministry across the board.

So I changed the main leadership role in music ministry to that of Band Leader. That structure exists to this day, and I have seen great fruit as people have appreciated the opportunity to put their efforts into seeing a band deliver great instrumental and vocal support to the congregational singing.

Where possible, I would suggest that churches attempt to recruit Band Leaders. A Music Director may well play the role of Band Leader for those bands that do not have a dedicated person. But where there is a dedicated person, the role of Music Director is slightly different.

As Music Director, instead of directing the majority of rehearsals, I will either absent myself from the band, or if I am needed to play or sing, I will do so in a way that reinforces the leadership of the Band Leader. I expand on this below, but in this setting, I will usually:

- Address any suggestions I may have for how things could sound to the Band Leader, not to the individual players (it shows band members that I am not the one calling all the shots)
- Make a point of asking the Band Leader if they have any objection to my giving specific performance suggestions to another member of the band (it shows the Band Leader respect for their role)

2. Getting the right people (recruiting leaders)

Who then should lead? How can they best be brought on board and brought up to speed? If you do not already have leaders, I would suggest making this a discussion topic for your next catch-up with your minister or supervisor. This will encourage the investment in your leaders to be shared. Thinking together about leaders is a crucial way of demonstrating that you wish your goals for music to line up with the priorities of your church's leadership.

Think together about who could best be encouraged to step up and take responsibility within your ministry. Remember that when asking anyone to serve in Christ's church, you are asking the person to serve Christ himself. This is nothing from which to shy away.

For a role such as a Band Leader, or an overseer of Band Leaders, consider giftedness in three crucial areas:

1. Christian example
2. Leadership skills
3. Musical skills.

People chosen for leadership may not necessarily be your most gifted players or vocalists. Indeed their leadership skills themselves might need honing. But I encourage you to have high expectations of their Christian example: look for the demonstration of the Spirit's work in their lives, and the affirmation by others of that person's suitability for the leadership role on view.

Having said this, our expectations of someone's Christian maturity may vary according to their age and stage in life. If I am to pick a leader for a youth band, I may have different expectations of that person's life maturity than I would have for a song leader for our family service.

The initial recruitment conversation with a prospective leader will unavoidably establish expectations for both the recruiter and recruit about what a leadership role will look like. If it is done poorly, you will feel like you are forever shaking off the effects of ambiguous communication. I therefore do not recommend email, SMS, or any other kind of messaging technology for this. The phone can work, but only when circumstances prevent a face-to-face.

The key points to establish when recruiting someone to a role are:

1. The goals or strategies of the music ministry broadly
2. The leadership roles (or other responsibilities) that you believe to be crucial to bringing these goals about

3. The person's suitability, in your eyes (and others' if appropriate) for a particular role, on the grounds of giftedness and Christian example
4. The details of what they would be responsible for
5. The person to whom they would be responsible and how that accountability would play out[9]

Do not underestimate the value of clear, upfront communication. Those amongst your people who value a well-organised structure with clear expectations will appreciate your efforts. They will lock these things away and will anticipate that their ongoing involvement will occur within these parameters.

But what about those who tend to prefer a more open-ended approach which evolves over time? Many of the musicians I have worked with over the years have preferred a more fluid approach (myself included at times). Perhaps this gives us a sense of not being stuck in a system.

We indeed should avoid creating anything that feels like a stifling system. However clear structures should really be about good relationships. I cannot properly manage a large team of musicians unless I am able to hold to account those people given the privilege of leadership. I need to be able to:

- Ask questions about aspects of our ministry that need addressing
- Give unsolicited feedback to leaders about how things are going when they are leading our church's music, including constructive criticism
- Ask how I may more effectively support them in the tasks for which I have recruited them.

3. The "catch-up" (following up consistently)

In my setting, which involves nine bands usually playing each

---

9 If you wished to develop your structure even further, you would add specific measures for how improvement would be tracked against those goals or strategies. Ultimately if measures for our goals are not identified, it is unlikely that there will be significant improvement against those goals. However, this can happen after the initial recruitment.

month, and one or two additional ensembles on top of that, there is potentially a great deal of leadership follow-up to be done. There is not always a Band Leader for each group, but nevertheless it is a big potential expenditure of time.

Having said that, I am a full time Music Director, which enables me to catch up with all my leaders on some kind of regular basis. For experienced leaders, this might be once per term or once per semester. For less experienced leaders, I aim to catch up monthly. Realistically it varies according to the ebb and flow of people's calendars, but having some kind of consistency works better for following up on their responsibilities than an ad hoc approach.

When a catch up occurs monthly, ideally for 90 minutes, I will try to include the following:

1. Personal questions: how is the person managing? Are any significant issues being faced in life generally?
2. A review of the most recent occasion on which the person led the band (see below for more detail about musical feedback).
3. Reflections on growth opportunities for both the leader and the members.
4. Song choices for the next occasion on which the person will lead, which includes a reasonably detailed discussion of the Bible passage to be preached.

So these catch up meetings are intended to keep on the agenda the key things about leadership: their Christian example, developing their leadership skills and their musical skills. But on top of this, I want my leaders to develop skills of biblical understanding and application. These skills are at the heart of song choosing, which is at the heart of all music ministry.

Not every Band Leader wants to do song choosing in our catch-ups, but many of the younger leaders are not only keen to learn about handling the Bible well, but also keen to contribute to the development of the song repertoire and to learn how to choose songs in a way that is both theologically and pastorally well considered.

When they are keen, I am delighted. I cannot think of a better way to give a young music leader a sense of what it is that we are doing than to open the Bible together to the passage that will be preached on when they next pull their band together. We can think and talk about what we will sing and why. Yes, I want to increase their sense of ownership of what will happen in those services. But there is actually an even greater goal.

Being a music leader is not about being the person with the most skills and insights. It is much more like pastoral word-based ministry than most people realize. If you sign up to being a Bible study leader or a youth leader, you should grow to understand that pastoring people is about letting God lead them. It is about reminding them that they are God's flock and that by sitting under his word, he will protect and guide them for all eternity.

Well, music ministry is also a pastoral ministry. Song writers summarise, quote and apply the word of God in the songs they write. That is a process of careful selection of words. But so too is song choosing. When we sing biblically based songs in church, we are taught, encouraged, challenged, made wise, and trained in righteousness. Both the selection of the repertoire or pool of songs as well as the selection of a song for a particular place in a particular service are extremely important ministries that music leaders (and their ministers) should treat with the utmost seriousness.

In choosing songs together, I push leaders hard in their understanding of the Bible, and do not let them get away with easy answers. My approach would be similar if I were catching up with a Bible study leader to help prepare for an upcoming study, except that instead of focusing on questions to ask and ways of guiding conversation, we are focusing on the songs that we will sing and the best ways to encourage the gatherings to embrace the content.

4. (My preferred method for) guiding musically

As I write this, I am 'multi-tasking'. I am sitting in the church building and listening to a rehearsal, tapping away on my laptop. In-between sentences for this chapter, I am writing down in another document my reflections on how things are sounding in the rehearsal.

The Band Leader is running the rehearsal. I am trying to analyse and evaluate, and I will send my comments on an email, which will then form the basis of a discussion when we catch up in a couple of weeks' time. I may also be able to send a recording of how it sounded to help refresh our memories for the discussion.

This process has two benefits (the feedback, not the multi-tasking!):

1. It gives the Band Leader an opportunity to try things and to grow through experience. It is easy for a Music Director like myself to feel the need to make every decision, and be involved in every aspect of the work or ministry. This is affectionately known as micromanaging… although people who have leadership responsibilities under this kind of oversight do not usually think of it "affectionately".

We do not need to control all the details in order to bring about our goals. What we need, if we wish to bring about goals, is people. And we only inhibit people's ability to contribute well (and their own personal growth) if we try to control them.

Many of our musicians have ideas that they would like to try out some time. Sometimes that is one of the drivers for wanting to become a leader. Creative passion needs an outlet.

Others need to be nudged to try things or make suggestions. They have latent skills that may flourish in an empowering environment. Most teams of church musicians that I have met have included both types. Both need to be enabled.

2. My feedback process encourages accountability. The Band Leader knows that we will chat about some of his or her musical decisions or leadership style later and so will try to get the most out of people and make the music sound as good as possible, appropriately tweaked for the congregational praise environment in which we serve. He or she is carefully listening to everything, knowing that I am listening too, and that I might comment on any of the instruments or vocalists and the contributions they are making.

If the Music Director is also a member of the band, it is harder for the Band Leader to take responsibility. The leader will usually assume that I will speak up if I have ideas or if something is not as good as it could be. To be brutally honest, a leader does not need to think quite so hard because it does not matter as much. Any ideas that are not particularly good can be easily run past me or modified by me before it is too late. Consequently, if I am in the band but do not modify something that I actually do feel could be improved, the leader will be under the impression that everything is fine. The Music Director has not said anything. So, since the person is shielded from the consequences of decisions, the weight of responsibility is reduced and there is less personal commitment.

It is not as if a Band Leader would receive any retribution or insult in my feedback. My goal is to emphasize positive elements as much as possible, and only give negative comments in a way that encourages the person to think of it as an opportunity for improvement. I will always identify more positive aspects than negative. In fact, my intention is usually to try to surprise them with strengths that they are unaware of.

Now I must also say that I would warn against doing this every time a person leads, because that might foster a sense of being micro-managed. I also do not do this without specifically asking the person in advance whether they would like this kind of feedback for a particular rehearsal coming up, or if they would prefer a more informal approach. Either works in my experience. However, good leaders always seem to be keen for feedback on how they are managing. And every time I have sent written feedback, the recipients have expressed their appreciation, and have often tried to clarify details or ask for suggestions of a way forward for improving in various areas.

The sorts of musical areas I will try to give feedback on are contained in these sorts of questions:
- How well do the key rhythm instruments reflect and reinforce the appropriate rhythm patterns for each song, particularly the main sub-divisions (i.e. is it quarter notes, 8s, or 16s if it is duple time, or is it 3|4 or 6|8 in triple time, and does it swing or is it straight in its feel?) and appropriate accents?
- How complementary were the parts played on key rhythm

instruments and did they work together or against each other?
- How effective was the use of counter melody by either melodic instruments, pitched rhythm instruments or vocalists?
- How appropriate was the choice of sounds or tone selected by each instrument? (i.e. keyboard players sometimes need guidance about using either rhythmic or non-rhythmic patches, and especially when to use background pads; electric guitarists sometimes need guidance about the right amount of overdrive, delay, as well as the twang or mellowness of their tone)
- How might the individuals in the band be most effectively encouraged, both to affirm them and get the best out of them?
- Are there aspects about the overall sound of the music that are especially pleasing, such as a particular person's voice quality or musical ability that could be nurtured and possibly featured at times?
- Are there particular problems that need a difficult conversation (which might be the Music Director's to have rather than the Band Leader's) such as the persistent tuning problems of instruments, the pitching issues with vocalists, or the stability of the tempo for a drummer or percussion player?
- How appropriate are the performance expectations placed on individual members in terms of their levels of skill and confidence? (Should an individual be nurtured within the safe environment of everyone playing together, or are they capable of a challenging song introduction on their own? Are there individuals who should be pushed out of their comfort zones in order to develop?)
- What encouragement can be given to the Band Leader about leadership style and the process of interacting with people in the running of rehearsals

5. Empowering experienced leaders

Although I often spend a greater proportion of my time with younger leaders, those with more experience are vital to our music ministries too, providing us with particular opportunities, and often challenges. Maturity and experience are goals for all of the members of the music team. And so when we are blessed with members who have decades under their belts, we should do our best to release their potential in our activities.

To empower the experienced, nurturing mutual respect is the crucial factor. We treat everyone in our teams with respect, of course. But if there are those in my team who have been part of many music teams before, or who have led a music ministry themselves, or who have a professional interest in music or ministry, it is particularly important for me to validate that experience.

This of course involves spending time one-on-one and showing a genuine and ongoing interest in the other person's background. Not only is it an act of love to show an interest in someone's background, it will make a person feel understood and appreciated, and it will encourage them to flourish. Not only this, I am always likely to learn something from their experience, even if it is quite different from my own.

Most importantly, giving large wads of detailed feedback to someone with extensive experience in church music may not be the best way to demonstrate respect. With experienced leaders, the emphasis should be on clarifying what it is we are trying to do and why, and then asking them for their ideas on how to achieve those goals.

Singing in church is not rocket science, and yet it is possible to get involved in detailed and nuanced conversations about what is important. We can find ourselves making assumptions about things that matter and disagreeing on things that are less significant in the long run. Experienced leaders tend to have strongly held views if they have invested greatly in music ministry in the past. Therefore, think generously about what points you want to insist on, and go easy in other areas. It is usually much better to have the experienced person on board, in partnership with you, helping you to work towards the goals than to have him or her feeling a little disenfranchised, wondering if their gifts might be better used in a different church.

Nevertheless, it is still important to give honest feedback. Experienced leaders are not exempt from the same expectations as anyone else in the music team. If anything, their example is observed more keenly than the example of younger leaders, and is certainly observed keenly by younger leaders.

If it is difficult to give feedback to younger, developing leaders, then it can be even more difficult to give feedback to the more experienced. My approach to this type of feedback is to limit it to the most important subjects. Whereas with a younger leader I will tend to go into a fair amount of detail about a band sound, with an experienced person I will tend to be more succinct, assuming that they understand what I am talking about. For example, I can simply say, "I wonder if the rhythm wasn't quite gelling", or "I think the vocalists need particular attention because they were missing cues and getting a few notes wrong". I may not need to go into the exact detail of the problem, because I am asking the leader to pay careful attention to a general point next time. I am effectively saying that I think that he or she has the ability to fix this, but for one reason or another may not have realized that there were issues.

The person may of course ask me for more details so that they can understand, or they may feel defensive (which may be understandable if it directly involves him or her). I believe that even if you do not give examples when you raise the issue, you should have a few examples up your sleeve in the event that he or she asks you to clarify what you have said or be more specific.

Empowering for team growth

This chapter has focused on the idea of empowerment as a key driver of team growth. The idea of empowerment sounds to some a little worldly. But there is a thoroughly gospel-shaped empowerment on view in 2 Timothy 2:2, where Paul encourages his protégé Timothy to *entrust the gospel to faithful and reliable people*. In serving in music in church, we have a gospel ministry. We need to consider which faithful and reliable people we will seek to raise up to be skilled in the use of music as a way of carrying the gospel to generations that follow.

It is not a do-as-you-please empowerment. We hand on clear goals and boundaries. Our ministry does much more than simply minimise distractions, and yet we need to be very well versed indeed in what those distractions are. As a leader, you need in your head a clear picture of what you would like your music ministry to become over time, and how you want your team to participate in working towards that picture.

Nevertheless, empowerment requires releasing control over many details of how things are done, while still giving leaders a clear sense of the essentials: that which must not be compromised. It requires giving your people a degree of latitude in how they do those things within the safe boundaries of these essentials.

As people kick goals together, their sense of shared purpose grows. So let's build a team of trusted people who know the difference between what is core and what is optional. Let's raise them up to reinforce the essential. In fact, I should encourage my leaders to do a whole range of things differently from how I myself would do them in the non-essential areas, since it will only point more clearly to what is consistent in our respective approaches to what is essential.

THE FIVE DOT-POINTS OF GOOD FEEDBACK

Andy Judd

Giving feedback is an important part of developing any ministry – we all know that. But a culture of good feedback giving (and receiving!) doesn't spring up overnight. Nobody likes receiving negative feedback. And people rarely know how to package up their feedback in a way that respects the other person while still making clear the areas of potential growth.

I've found having a model for feedback which all my leaders are familiar with helps hugely with the potential for awkwardness or unhelpfulness. Most people go with the "poo sandwich" model of feedback (one nice thing, then one bad thing, then one nice then). Everybody sees through this. They know (or think they know) that what you "really think" is coming in the middle. Personally, I can't stand this way of getting or giving feedback.

A much better model, I find, is to have these five points to go through in order.[10] They work for pretty much anything you might be giving feedback on:

1. What were you trying to do?
2. If that's what you were trying to do, then what do you think went well?
3. If that's what you were trying to do, then what do you think needs to be different or better?
4. Here's what I think needed to be different or better.
5. Here's what I think you did well.

---

[10] I should say that this model for feedback is hardly original. It is influenced by two sources: (1) the insightful mentoring of consultant Peter Stone, and (2) the very helpful coaching and review tool from Moore College's Centre for Ministry Development (**https://cmd.moore.edu.au/Media/Default/Resources/Coaching%20method%20-%20CMD.pdf**)

Steve Crain and Andy Judd

CHAPTER EIGHT: Auditions and skill levels

Church bands are a wonderful opportunity for musicians to be the gift to the church that God has made them to be. We want every musician to be developing their skills, at whatever stage they are currently at.

On the other hand, we should not expect everybody to have the skills required to be a blessing to the church on any given instrument.

Setting the balance between these two is one of the trickiest parts of forming a church music culture. This can lead to tensions within churches as differing cultures collide:

- In a small church service where everyone knows each other, their culture emphasises a willingness to serve over giftedness.
- In a large church service where most people do not know the musician on stage, their culture places more emphasis on musical gifts and character.

Neither of these cultures is necessarily wrong (although we can imagine unhelpful extremes in each case). They are simply adapted to the church they are in. The problem comes when there is a lack of clarity about the culture and the reasons for it.

- If I come from a small church culture I may be shocked and offended at the suggestion that I should "audition" for the band: "it's not about the performance, it's about the heart!"
- If I come from a large church, I may look down on the unprofessionalism and apparently low standard of a small church music team: "Don't you guys care?!"

At Barneys Broadway, in Sydney, we feel this tension all the time as students coming to Sydney for study move from small church music cultures to a medium sized church music culture. That's one of the reasons we have a really clear audition process.

Why we do auditions

Clear expectations right from the start save a world of pain down the line: that's why we have decided to have an audition process for musician in our Sunday service teams. We try to be up front and transparent about the minimum standard of musicianship required to play at one of our main services. Of course this standard is, in some ways, fairly arbitrary, and we've found it can even vary depending on the requirements of our different services.

There are three added benefits of an audition process:

First, having auditions lets us determine a person's strengths and weaknesses so we can roster well-structured bands. This really helps both the auditionee not be thrown in the deep end, and helps us balance bands so that less gifted players are not put under pressure by other less gifted players. For example, some singers need very clear introductions so they can feel secure to lead the congregation to the best of their ability. But if a pianist who cannot yet provide an introduction of the required standard is rostered on with them then both the singer and the in turn the pianist will probably feel the serving experience has been a negative one, not a positive one.

Second, by examining people's strengths and weaknesses we will be better able to talk about how to develop their gift, which this model assumes is a Christian's desire. We can potentially offer training seminars tailored to people's needs, suggest training materials they can study (books, CDs, DVDs), and set goals to help them achieve the development of their gifts.

Third, the audition process allows us to have a one to one chat about a person's background in serving in music, and have a conversation about what they can expect from us, and we what will be expect from them. We ask questions like:

- What has your involvement in church been so far? Which service do you normally attend?

- What previous experience do you have? Do you sing? Which instruments do you play?
- What made you want to audition for the music team?
- Have you prayerfully considered the time and commitment that is required to steward your gift well?

The audition process

Everyone who wants to join the music team is given detailed information about the audition process, as well as sheet music for the song we'll ask them to play and a document which explains our music vision. If they decide they're happy going through with it, they can then arrange a time for an audition.

Depending on the day, this might be a small group audition (for example, with two or three other singers who are also auditioning at the same time) or a solo audition. It is sometimes run by the music director, but if he can't make it we have some experienced members of the music team who have been trained up to run auditions. They record the audition for the music director to listen back to later.

After beginning with prayer, we then sing or play through a familiar song from our repertoire together with the person running the audition. If it's a drummer auditioning solo then the person running the audition might jump on bass guitar to play along with them. If it's a group vocal audition the person running the audition might get each person to sing through the melody of the verse and chorus individually, then sing through the chorus while the leader sings a harmony, and then sing a harmony of their own. After the audition we pray again, and then everyone goes home (or grabs a coffee).

After the audition we prepare each person written feedback and then set up a time to go through it with them. This requires everyone to bring a humble attitude of service, hold their gifts loosely, understand the concept of 'gift stewardship' and have an ability to give and receive constructive criticism.

It is important to be clear that this process does not end after the audition. If a person's gifting is not yet at the level that we have set for regular inclusion in the team for services, then we endeavor to explain why we see it that way, and what we feel will need to be developed before the person will be included. As you can imagine, these conversations are potentially awkward (they sure are for me!). But avoiding honest conversations because we fear a person's reaction (either them getting hurt or them not liking us) is not a good way to operate in Christian community. We need to trust that God knows what He is doing by setting it up this way. While it is a scary process to go through, it is certainly an opportunity for us to stand out as different from the world (just watch some Australian Idol auditions!).

The goal is to try to work out where they are at as a musician, what things they could improve on, and whether they are ready to start playing (and in which context). For that, we have the musician levels sheets.

Musician levels sheets

These 'levels' sheets were developed to help identify a musician's current level of competency in as objective and encouraging a way as possible.

Level one for each instrument is intended as a basic level of competency required to play in a church band. If, after a relaxed informal audition, a musician doesn't seem to have level one nailed, it's not the end of the road. Book a follow up audition for a month's time and give them some guidance about what to work on.

If the musician has level one together, they can start playing at church. But that's not the end of the road either – the levels sheet can give them guidance about what they need to do to get to the next level.

These levels sheets were originally created by Steve Crain (and Andrew Massey in the case of the drum levels) and subsequently developed by Curtis Smith and Andy Judd.

Note: It is entirely appropriate that different churches will have different standards for their musicians. These standards might vary depending on the demands placed on their musicians in a given service (number of songs, rehearsal time, size of repertoire), the size of the church, the style of music played and the expectations of the congregation.

Drum levels

A level one player should be able to:
- [ ] understand basic stick grip and stroke
- [ ] know and play combinations of quarter, eighth and sixteenth notes
- [ ] play a basic rock beat
- [ ] play at least one fill around the kit
- [ ] play a combination of 3 bars beat + 1 bar fill without losing time
- [ ] demonstrate a single stroke roll

A level two player should be able to:
- [ ] know and play combinations of quarter, eighth and sixteenth notes and their associated rests
- [ ] play one half-time beat and a triplet or 6/8 beat
- [ ] play at least four different fills around the kit
- [ ] play a whole song length (including beats and fills) without losing time
- [ ] demonstrate a single stroke roll, double stroke roll and paradiddle
- [ ] play a syncopated pattern on snare with quarter notes on bass drum
- [ ] know the form of a song

A level three player should be able to:
- [ ] play a variety of rock & dance beats, including a 2 handed hi-hat beat and open hi-hat techniques
- [ ] play several types of fills around the kit (using whole, half, quarter, eighth, and sixteenth notes and their rests)
- [ ] play five whole songs (including beats and fills) with other musicians and to a metronome without losing time
- [ ] read important sections of the chart
- [ ] count the band in
- [ ] show good ensemble skills (write out drum parts, create parts with bass player, use of dynamics, cue sections of song)

A level four player should be able to:
- [ ] know and play combinations of quarter, eighth, sixteenth, and thirty-second notes and their associated rests
- [ ] play advanced beats in any time signature
- [ ] play several types of fill around the kit (using whole, half, quarter, eighth, sixteenth, and thirty-second notes and their rests)
- [ ] demonstrate a single stroke roll, double stroke roll, 5-stroke roll, 7-stroke roll, 9-stroke roll and use on kit to a metronome
- [ ] write and read a comprehensive chart
- [ ] demonstrate the ability to solo over sections of a song

Keyboard levels

A level one player should be able to:
- [ ] turn the keyboard on, get basic sounds (piano, organ, electric piano, pad), plug into amp, attach damper/sustain pedal
- [ ] read major and minor chord symbols
- [ ] tap foot and count out loud
- [ ] stay in time with a drummer
- [ ] sit on their left hand (to keep out of the bass player's way)
- [ ] play eggs (one chord per bar)
- [ ] play minums (two chords per bar)
- [ ] play basic syncopated rhythms
- [ ] understand slash chords (e.g. A/C#, G/B)
- [ ] read a chart without disaster (repeats, 1st and 2nd time bars, sign, coda)

A level two player should be able to:
- [ ] quickly voice all major and minor chords in all keys in various inversions (either hand)
- [ ] pick suitable voicings for the song (Voice leading, guide tones, etc)
- [ ] add Sus 2 and Sus 4 to chord voicings
- [ ] layer sounds (i.e. add strings to piano)
- [ ] play with a better sense of time (setting and maintaining solid tempo without drummer)
- [ ] play basic "Imagine" broken chord groove (4 to the bar)
- [ ] give clear and helpful prompts to singers (entrances, key changes etc)
- [ ] not play sometimes

A level three player should be able to:
- [ ] play major, minor and dominant 7th chords, in various voicings (inversions)
- [ ] move between chords melodically (tension and release, 'probing', etc)
- [ ] improvise on major and minor pentatonic scales and use these in fills
- [ ] nail standard rhythmic patterns
- [ ] play with even better sense of time
- [ ] create parts which fit well with other instruments
- [ ] play differently for different sounds (organ, electric piano, strings, etc)
- [ ] play with light and shade (build excitement, pull back, without changing tempo)
- [ ] follow vocalists in intros etc. (good *cola voce* ability)
- [ ] play four part traditional hymns with minimal practice

Chapter EIGHT: Auditions and skill levels

A level four player should be able to:

- [ ] improvise tasteful melodies in gaps (soloing), understanding modes, chord theory and the principle of tension/release
- [ ] play with fantastic sense of time and feel, either with or without other instruments
- [ ] keep a solid technique (totally independent hands, smooth touch, control of dynamics, accuracy, etc.)
- [ ] hear chords and notes on the fly (great relative or absolute pitch)
- [ ] create amazing parts which fit with the other instruments and serve the songs
- [ ] create sounds which fit your parts and sounds perfectly (know your gear, programming, organ drawbars, effects)
- [ ] write charts out (e.g. condense long charts down to a one pager)
- [ ] understand advanced chord theory (jazz stuff)
- [ ] sight-read four part traditional hymn charts
- [ ] improvise using a very broad repertoire of rhythmic parts (comping patterns)

Electric guitar levels

A level one player should be able to:
- [ ] tune up including using tuner and volume pedal
- [ ] get a basic sound (using the church gear or their own rig)
- [ ] play open chord shapes
- [ ] play power chords on E and A
- [ ] strum a basic pattern (12&&4 - dduud)
- [ ] tap foot and count out loud
- [ ] play eggs (whole notes)
- [ ] play minums
- [ ] play on/off 1 &
- [ ] read a chart without catastrophe (repeats, 1st and 2nd time bars, sign, coda)
- [ ] understand what slash chords mean (A/C#, G/B etc)

A level two player should be able to:
- [ ] play triads on top 3 strings
- [ ] play triads on next 3 strings
- [ ] play arpeggios over basic 3 chord progressions 1&2& etc
- [ ] play a funky strumming pattern e.g. Dr Feelgood
- [ ] voice chords
- [ ] voice regular slash chords E/G#, G/B, A/C#, F/G, A/G
- [ ] play more advanced open chords G5, C2, F2
- [ ] pull up intermediate sounds
- [ ] play with a better sense of time

A level three player should be able to:
- [ ] play octaves
- [ ] play minor pentatonic shapes
- [ ] play major pentatonic shapes
- [ ] voice Sus2 triads
- [ ] play plinky parts
- [ ] understand theory of triads
- [ ] understand diatonic harmony and apply it to tunes
- [ ] play with very good sense of time

Chapter EIGHT: Auditions and skill levels

A level four player should be able to:
- [ ] read music well
- [ ] improvise a solo over chord changes
- [ ] pull advanced sounds
- [ ] play chord melody
- [ ] play great intros
- [ ] understand four note chord theory
- [ ] condense large charts to 1 or 2 pages
- [ ] recognise chord progressions by ear
- [ ] play with fantastic sense of time

Acoustic guitar levels

A level one player should be able to:
- [ ] tune up including using tuner and volume pedal/DI
- [ ] play open chord shapes
- [ ] play power chords on E & A and barre chords
- [ ] strum a basic pattern (e.g. 1 2& &4 – d du ud)
- [ ] play 1 strum/2 strums per bar while staying in time
- [ ] tap foot and count out loud
- [ ] read a chart without cataclysm (repeats, first/second time bars, sign, coda)
- [ ] understand slash chords

A level two player should be able to:
- [ ] play arpeggios over basic 3 chord progressions
- [ ] strum advanced patterns (sixteenth notes)
- [ ] play advanced open chords (G5, C2, F2, D2, D5)
- [ ] voice slash chords (E/G#, F/A, Bm/A, A/C#, D/C, G/B, A/G, C/G, Am/G, Dm/C)
- [ ] mute low E string for open chords with A or D string roots (e.g. C, A, D, B7)
- [ ] know basic chord theory (major and minor triad formulas and major scales numbers)
- [ ] play one major scale shape
- [ ] play with solid time feel (e.g. intros, breakdowns)
- [ ] use a capo (take home chart and write out capo chords)

A level three player should be able to:
- [ ] play open string drone voicings (E, A and D strings)
- [ ] play E string root 1735 voicings
- [ ] play other major scale shapes
- [ ] perform 'Walkdowns' using slash chords in G, D, C (eg: G, D/F#, Em, Em/D, C2, G/B, Bm/A)
- [ ] play major/minor pentatonic shapes
- [ ] voice Sus2 triads
- [ ] understand triad theory and diatonic harmony, and apply to tunes
- [ ] use capo automatically (converting chords to numbers in order to transpose on the spot)
- [ ] understand how to work together with a second acoustic guitar

Chapter EIGHT: Auditions and skill levels

A level four player should be able to:
- ☐ improvise a decent solo
- ☐ play a chord based melody (e.g. intros)
- ☐ understand four note chord theory
- ☐ voice other four note chords off A and D strings (1573, 1357)
- ☐ use open tunings
- ☐ recognise chord progressions by ear
- ☐ play with fantastic sense of time

Bass

A level one player should be able to:
- [ ] know all the notes on neck up to 5th position
- [ ] play basic grooves (1, 2&) (1, 2&, 3) (1&2&3&4&)
- [ ] get a basic tone
- [ ] tune the instrument well
- [ ] read a basic chord chart

A level two player should be able to:
- [ ] know all the notes on neck
- [ ] play major and minor arpeggios
- [ ] play major pentatonic simple fills
- [ ] play with consistent note length and consistent tone
- [ ] navigate more advanced chord charts (sign, coda, repeats, 1st & 2nd time bars)
- [ ] play more syncopated rhythms (16th note off beats)
- [ ] read hymns and left hand of piano parts
- [ ] hear a drummer's part and play a relevant and consistent groove
- [ ] keep their head up, listening in to band playing

A level three player should be able to:
- [ ] use a wider range on the bass (higher parts/more melodic parts)
- [ ] control their tone and volume with high degree of sensitivity
- [ ] connect sections of songs / chords
- [ ] use other techniques (slapping/muting/effects) appropriately
- [ ] play with very strong time feel (e.g. when playing as solo accompaniment)
- [ ] be highly aware of other instruments parts and choose relevant styles and voice bass parts

A level four player should be able to:
- [ ] lead the band with your part, through decisive and strong playing
- [ ] solo over any material required
- [ ] have intimate knowledge of note choices substitutions and re-harmonisation
- [ ] memorise material quickly and easily

Single note instrument (violin etc) levels

A level one player should be able to:
- [ ] understand the role of a single note instrument in a band
- [ ] play with accurate pitch
- [ ] play guide tones (e.g. minims and semibreves)
- [ ] read a chart (repeats, first and second time bars, sign, coda)
- [ ] play a simple melody (supporting an existing melody)

A level two player should be able to:
- [ ] understand basic chord theory (diatonic chords and numbers)
- [ ] play advanced guide tones (quarter notes)
- [ ] improvise ornamental 'fills' (especially between lyrics)
- [ ] play major pentatonic and major scales
- [ ] play a solo melody (intro/instrumental)
- [ ] form a whole song concept (using melody, guide tones, silence appropriately)

A level three player should be able to:
- [ ] understand advanced chord theory, including knowing all notes in all major & minor triads
- [ ] play advanced fills ('letting rip' in climax of a song)
- [ ] play minor pentatonic scales, blues scales.
- [ ] harmonise a melody
- [ ] wide use of the instrument's range (violin's neck etc.)
- [ ] coordinate with the electric guitar

A level four player should be able to:
- [ ] improvise an advanced tasteful solo, using principles of tension/release
- [ ] adapt to a variety of styles including blues, country, pop, classical
- [ ] perform advanced fills (using sixteenth notes)
- [ ] tasteful and sensitive understanding of role of a their instrument in a contemporary worship band

Vocalist levels

A level one vocalist should be able to:
- [ ] understand the role of a vocalist in leading singing in church
- [ ] sing with consistently accurate pitch and suitable vocal range
- [ ] sing with good and consistent time (not rushing accompaniment etc.)
- [ ] sing with clear tone, blending well with other singers
- [ ] hold a melody while someone else sings a harmony
- [ ] read a chart (repeats, first and second time bars, sign, coda) and confidently lead vocal entries
- [ ] use a microphone with proper technique, including rolling cables and setting up microphone on stand

A level two vocalist should be able to:
- [ ] very good pitch, tone and vocal control (tasteful vibrato, air support etc)
- [ ] learn and sing a basic harmony
- [ ] present and lead the congregation confidently
- [ ] introduce songs with appropriate words
- [ ] communicate with the band during performances, and respond to unexpected 'changes'
- [ ] know how to ask for the foldback they need to do their job

A level three vocalist should be able to:
- [ ] excellent pitch, tone and vocal control
- [ ] develop a harmony and teach it to other vocalists
- [ ] understand the flow of the service and adapt accordingly
- [ ] 'read' the congregation and help lead them musically and spiritually through the service
- [ ] take responsibility for everything they need to perform well in challenging situations (microphones, foldback, etc)

Andy Judd

CHAPTER NINE: Emotional manipulation

There is a great deal of suspicion of emotional manipulation. Sometimes I think that suspicion is justified. A friend told me a story about a church where the keyboard was hooked up to an electric shock machine, and just at the right moment the keyboard player would hit the button and people in the front row would be brought to their knees by the 'electrifying' power of the sermon.

But sometimes I wonder whether we are oversensitive to the power of music on our emotions, as if being moved emotionally by a song is less 'worthy' of us than to be moved intellectually by a sermon.

Consider the tension felt by the great father of the faith, Augustine. His conversion story was marked by an emotional musical encounter:

> "I wept at your [God's] hymns and canticles, deeply moved by the voices of your sweetly singing church. Those voices flowed into my ears, and the truth was poured out in my heart, whence a feeling of piety surged up and my tears ran down. And these things were good for me."[1]

Yet at the same time, the Platonism which Augustine's culture had subscribed to made him suspicious of such animal attraction merely based on music:

> "the gratification of my flesh – to which I ought not to surrender my mind to be enervated – frequently leads my astray ... when it happens to me that the song moves me more than the thing which is sung, I confess that I have sinned blamefully and then prefer not to hear the singer.[2]

For similar reasons, another thinker, Athanasius, decided that it would be better not to sing at all. For him it was important that the Psalms were recited not 'from a desire for pleasing sound', but as a more spiritual 'manifestation of harmony among the thoughts of the soul'.[3] Augustine, to his credit, didn't go that far. But he did look down on the role of music, saying it merely enabled a 'weaker soul' to 'be elevated to an attitude of devotion'.[4]

But I don't think it is an admission of weakness in our soul to recognise that we are *embodied*: our thoughts and actions are influenced by what we eat, whether we have slept enough recently, and whether our brain chemicals are balanced. To recognise that music can have a non-rational effect on our souls is simply to recognise that we are human. Rather than be afraid of *any* emotional effect, we should seek out music which draws us closer to God and honours Jesus. Provided there is no deception, and the emotional power of the music is anchored in the truth, and we aren't trying to substitute for the Spirit's work in changing hearts, I can't see the danger. If 'manipulation' means simply helping me to feel the weight of Jesus' glory then please, go ahead: some days I could do with a bit of musical manipulation.

1. Augustine, *Confessiones* IX, vi, 14 in James McKinnon, *Music in Early Christian Literature* (Cambridge: Cambridge University Press, 1989), 154.
2. Augustine, *Confessiones* X, xxxiii, 49-50 in McKinnon, *Music in Early Christian Literature*, 154.
3. Athanasius, *Epistula ad Marcellinum* 29, PG XXVII, 40-1 in McKinnon, *Music in Early Christian Literature*, 53.
4. Augustine, *Confessiones* X, xxxiii, 49-50 in McKinnon, *Music in Early Christian Literature*, 154.

Andy Judd

CHAPTER TEN: The lessons of history

In many church circles, 'worship' is synonymous with music: *worship pastors* wield guitars; *worship time* is when you dim the lights and power up the amplifiers. But this link between devotion to God and music (particularly instrumental music) is by no means obvious. Last month a friendly Imam from southwest Sydney offered to take me around his Mosque. He pointed out that our worship had much in common: prayer, exposition of scripture, ethical teaching and fellowship. But no music. I heard of a Christian convert to Islam whose first question was 'where is the organ?' They just laughed.

Christian worship has always been musical – yet Christians have seldom agreed on *why*. This chapter will survey the development of worship music theology by examining three influential thinkers: Augustine, Martin Luther and John Wesley. We will see that Christians have not simply developed their theologies of music in worship by grappling with scripture: they have often been *reactive*, defining themselves against the practices of groups they oppose. This has shaped their vision of music in worship, and not always constructively. Christians today from all traditions must evaluate and respond to the marketplace of worship theologies on offer; these examples from history are helpful in that task.

Early church

From Judaism the first Christians inherited a singing culture.[11] From the outset their God was very specific about how adherents should

---

11 Paul Bradshaw, *The Search for the Origins of Christian Worship: Sources and Methods for the Study of Early Liturgy* (2nd ed.; London: SPCK, 2002), 39.

worship him: no drawings, no sculptures and no carvings.[12] But they certainly could *sing* about him. When representing his glory, God prefers psalm to painting. So God's people have always sung. When God's mighty arm drew Israel out of Egypt, this nation-building act was answered by Miriam and Moses in songs of praise.[13] Later, as God laid down plans for temple worship, he made provisions for full time worship pastors: temple musicians from the tribe of Levi.[14]

We know little about how this music sounded, except that it probably involved some instruments, and that by David's time production values were high – Psalm 33, for example, enjoins skilful lyre playing.[15] The subtle images and delicate parallelisms of Old Testament lyrics offer glimpses at the artistic effort the Israelites poured into the words of their worship music.[16]

The early church continued singing: Paul and Silas sang in their Philippian gaol cell, and Paul implies that songs featured in Corinthian gatherings.[17] But early on the Church distinguished its singing from Jewish temple music with the absence of musical instruments. This was partly a reflection of synagogue practices.[18] Yet it was also a deliberate reaction against surrounding pagan cultures, which for them wreaked of unbridled sensuality and idolatry.[19] To guard morality and doctrine, Christian worship needed to be distinguished unambiguously from pagan practices. Clement of Alexandria (115–c216) advised believers to 'no longer employ the ancient psaltery, trumpet, timbrel, or flute',

---

12   Exodus 20:4, Leviticus 26:1.
13   Exodus 15.
14   2 Chronicles 5:12-14.
15   See also Psalm 150.
16   See Robert Alter, **The Art of Biblical Poetry** (New York: Basic Books, 1985).
17   Acts 16:25; 1 Corinthians 13:26.
18   See James McKinnon, 'The Meaning of Patristic Polemic Against Musical Instruments', in **Studies in Early Christianity** (ed. Everett Ferguson; New York: Garland, 1993), 291; Jeremy Begbie, **Resounding Truth: Christian Wisdom in the World of Music** (Grand Rapids: Baker Academic, 2007), 72.
19   Johannes Quasten, **Music and Worship in Pagan and Christian Antiquity** (Washington D.C.: National Association of Pastoral Musicians, 1983), 60; Eric Werner, 'Notes on the Attitude of the Early Church Fathers Towards Hebrew Psalmody', in **Studies in Early Christianity** (ed. Everett Ferguson; New York: Garland, 1993), 345.

which 'inflame desire, stir up lust, or arouse anger' (he did, on King David's account, make concession for the use of cithara and lyre at *agape* meals).[20] John Chrysostom (347-407) dismissed the musical instruments in the Psalms as, like cultic sacrifice, an accommodation to Israel's 'dull temperament'.[21] Christian worship music, for Chrysostom at least, would not involve individuals playing instruments, but a body of 'living strings' bound by the Spirit:

> Our tongues are the chords of the cithara which come forth as a diverse sound yet form a divine harmony. Women, men, the aged, youth, are all certainly individual persons, but they are not individuals when they sing hymns, for the Spirit, governing the voice of each, brings about one melody in all.[22]

Reacting against an ominous cultural threat, Christian worship theology developed its own 'sacred' style of *a cappella* music.[23]

Augustine

Born mid-fourth century, Augustine of Hippo is a towering figure in Christian thought. He reports in his most famous work, *Confessions*, how prior to his conversion the music of the church deeply moved him:

> I wept at your [God's] hymns and canticles, deeply moved by the voices of your sweetly singing church. Those voices flowed into my ears, and the truth was poured out in my heart, whence a feeling of piety surged up and my tears ran down. And these things were good for me.[24]

---

20 Clement of Alexander, 'The Tutor of Children', in Lawrence Johnson, ***Worship in the Early Church: An Anthology of Historical Sources*** (Minnesota: Liturgical Press, 2009), para 832; Quasten, ***Music and Worship in Pagan and Christian Antiquity***, 73.
21 John Chrysostom, 'On Psalm 149', in Johnson, ***Worship in the Early Church: Anthology of Historical Sources***, para 1470. Likewise Nicetas of Remesiana, 'On The Usefulness of Psalmody', para 3197.
22 John Chrysostom, 'On Psalm 145', in Johnson, ***Worship in the Early Church: Anthology of Historical Sources***, para 1469.
23 A cappella means without instruments, from the Italian for 'In the chapel style'.
24 Augustine, ***Confessiones*** IX, vi, 14 in James McKinnon, ***Music in Early Christian Literature*** (Cambridge: Cambridge University Press, 1989), 154.

Yet Augustine struggled to accommodate this formative experience of the emotional power of worship music within his theology. It may be that Plotinus' neo-Platonist tradition left many Christian thinkers, like Augustine, with a dim valuation of the physical world, giving priority to reason over emotions.[25] But Augustine worried that his response to Christian worship music might have more to do with the music than the truth it embodied:

> the gratification of my flesh – to which I ought not to surrender my mind to be enervated – frequently leads my astray ... when it happens to me that the song moves me more than the thing which is sung, I confess that I have sinned blamefully and then prefer not to hear the singer.[26]

Augustine was aware that Athanasius, the great defender of Trinitarian orthodoxy, was unenthusiastic about the emotional power of music. Athanasius reportedly thought it best if the singer only slightly inflected the words to make it closer to speaking than singing,[27] insisting that recitation of the Psalms 'is not done from a desire for pleasing sound, but is a manifestation of harmony among the thoughts of the soul'.[28] Athanasius thus outlawed the new style of melodic singing which appeared in the fourth to early fifth centuries, and ruled that only the very words of scripture should be sung in church.[29]

Yet something of Augustine's first moving experience of worship music restrained him from taking the hard line favoured by Athanasius. He admitted that there might be great benefit in the 'fluent voice and music that is most appropriate', though only because they might help

---

25 Everett Ferguson, *Backgrounds of Early Christianity* (3rd ed.; Grand Rapids: Eerdmans, 2003), 392.
26 Augustine, *Confessiones* X, xxxiii, 49-50 in McKinnon, *Music in Early Christian Literature*, 154.
27 William T. Flynn, 'Liturgical Music', in *The Oxford History of Christian Worship* (ed. Geoffrey Wainwright; Oxford: Oxford University Press, 2006), 775; Augustine, *Confessiones* X, xxxiii, 49-50 in McKinnon, *Music in Early Christian Literature*, 154.
28 Athanasius, *Epistula ad Marcellinum* 29, PG XXVII, 40-1 in McKinnon, *Music in Early Christian Literature*, 53.
29 Flynn, 'Liturgical Music', 775.

the 'weaker soul ... be elevated to an attitude of devotion'.[30] Music which reflected a sincere heart was allowed,[31] but only as a crutch for immature Christians.

Surveys can do little justice to the rich period following Augustine. Certainly, instruments were still mostly off limits until the end of the middle ages (some early organs notwithstanding). Likewise a general preference for scriptural texts and a suspicion of strong emotions continued through the middle ages. This bred art forms to match: the beautiful monophonic simplicity of the Gregorian chant, for instance, was designed to inspire serious spiritual contemplation.[32]

On the other hand, some writers from the period complained that increasingly complex harmony made it almost impossible to tell what language the singers were singing.[33] Pope John XXII was concerned enough about the development of polyphonic forms to try to limit its use.[34] But this did little to curtail the exploration of polyphonic possibilities throughout the Christian world.

This increasing complexity was meant to engage the faculties in apprehending the holiness of God, and anticipate heavenly worship. Yet the professionalism needed to pull it off left dwindling room for congregational involvement. While Tertullian hints that even in the early church songs were performed by individuals,[35] for writers like Ambrose of Milan, John Chrysostom and Basil the Great, the focus of church singing had always been communal.[36] Yet by the fifth century, some congregations were merely responding to cantillated (chanted) Psalm readings with the Alleluia (a practice called 'lector chant'); by the

---

30 Augustine, **Confessiones** X, xxxiii, 49-50 in McKinnon, **Music in Early Christian Literature**, 154.
31 Augustine, 'Rule of Saint Augustine', II.3 in Johnson, **Worship in the Early Church: Anthology of Historical Sources**, para 2599.
32 Evans, **Music in the Modern Church**, 27.
33 Evans, **Music in the Modern Church**, 28.
34 Evans, **Music in the Modern Church**, 27.
35 Flynn, 'Liturgical Music', 770.
36 John Chrysostom, 'On Psalm 145' at para 1469; Ambrose of Milan 'Commentaries on the Twelve Psalms of David' at para 1158; Basil the Great, 'Homily on Psalm 1' at para 1346, in Johnson, **Worship in the Early Church: Anthology of Historical Sources**.

tenth century the ordinary mass in many places was sung entirely by a choir of trained clergy called the *schola*.[37]

Luther

During the Renaissance, musical sophistication only increased. Composers like Josquin des Prez (1450-1521) thought music *itself* carried meaning, not just in the words but in the melody and harmonies, so lyrics and tunes needed to be matched carefully.[38] Furthermore the relationship between secular and sacred music became 'increasingly symbiotic'.[39] The protestant reformers thus inherited a complex musical tradition, many using music powerfully to promote their own theological positions.

But developments in protestant theologies of worship music were often reactive: like the church fathers, the reformers rejected the practices of opposing traditions in order to carve out their own unique identity. The French reformer John Calvin (1509–1564) was deeply suspicious of both the complex polyphonic music of the Catholic church, and the 'lascivious, injurious, alluring' secular music of the day.[40] He thus forbade anything that might obscure the meaning of the words, including harmonies and instruments. Polyphony was fine in private, but not in church.[41] But he was also wary of the *inherent* emotional power of music, worrying that 'venom and corruption' might reach 'the depths of the heart'.[42] The best safeguard was to limit singing to scripture. Calvinist services utilised the Genevan Psalter (1551) which set readable translations of the Psalms to pure and simple melodies.[43] Even more severe was the Swiss Ulrich Zwingli, whose belief that 'spirit and flesh contradict each other' cast doubt on singing as acceptable

---

37 Flynn, 'Liturgical Music', 771-3.
38 Evans, *Music in the Modern Church*, 29.
39 Evans, *Music in the Modern Church*, 29.
40 Charles Garside, *The Origins of Calvin's Theology of Music: 1536–1543* (Philadelphia: American Philosophical Society, 1979), 28.
41 Flynn, 'Liturgical Music', 782.
42 Paul Westermeyer, *Te Deum: The Church and Music* (Minneapolis: Fortress, 1998), 156.
43 Evans, *Music in the Modern Church*, 31.

worship.⁴⁴ Despite being an accomplished musician himself, Zwingli insisted that worship of God was to be inward: 'not with our voices, like the Jewish singers, but with our hearts'.⁴⁵ So when Zurich's clergy purged the city of relics and images in the summer of 1524, they incapacitated the organs as well.⁴⁶

But for German reformer Martin Luther (1483–1546), the problem with Renaissance worship music was not its instruments, but its poor instruction. A teacher by nature, he was concerned that music should instruct his congregations, particularly youth, in good doctrine. He believed that 'the way of the gospel led through the ear more than the eye.'⁴⁷ He wrote:

> 'For their sake [simple laymen] we must read, sing, preach, write and compose, and if it would help the matter along, I would have all the bells pealing, and all the organs playing, and let everything chime that has a clapper'.⁴⁸

Luther's tradition used Gregorian chant, sacred folk songs, instruments and occasionally the higher secular tunes: whatever musical vehicle would carry the truth most clearly.⁴⁹ It was only the *abuse* of the arts which needed to be opposed.⁵⁰ It was the Lutheran tradition that became home to a high water mark of the Baroque period: J. S. Bach flourished in St Thomas's Lutheran Church in Leipzig, Germany, under the influence of Luther's theology of worship music.

Luther prized scriptural words and ideas – for him the Holy Spirit was the greatest singer and poet of praise to God – but thought it more important to express the meaning of scripture than its words.⁵¹

---

44 Paul Westermeyer, *Te Deum: The Church and Music* (Minneapolis: Fortress, 1998), 151.
45 Ulrich Zwingli, 'Conclusion 45' in Charles Garside, *Zwingli and the Arts* (New Haven: Yale, 1966), 45.
46 Paul Westermeyer, *Te Deum: The Church and Music* (Minneapolis: Fortress, 1998), 150.
47 Vilmos Vajta, *Luther on Worship: An Interpretation* (trans. U.S. Leupold; Philadelphia: Muhlenberg, 1958), 185.
48 Flynn, 'Liturgical Music', 780.
49 Paul Westermeyer, *Te Deum: The Church and Music* (Minneapolis: Fortress, 1998), 148.
50 Vajta, *Luther on Worship*, 187.
51 Vajta, *Luther on Worship*, 161.

He also saw an urgent need to re-establish the communal dimension of worship singing. For Luther, the singing of praise was the means by which God becomes 'Our God', as we confess him the giver of all we prize most.[52] Such praise is therefore, for Luther, a profoundly corporate experience, unifying the church militant on earth with the church triumphant in heaven to praise God.[53]

Wesley

But in England, it was Calvin's position that held sway. 'Plain' and 'modest' songs in English language, with simple harmony, were mandated under Edward VI.[54] For Queen Elizabeth I, the emphasis was on intelligibility: there was to be 'a distinct modest song, so used in all parts of the common prayers in the church, that the same may be plainly understood, as if it were read without singing.'[55] A modest and plainly understood English Psalter was provided, with variable proficiency, by the sixteenth century compiler Thomas Sternhold.[56]

It was the non-conformists, reacting against what they saw as stifling English worship, that gave us the great hymn writers of the eighteenth century. Isaac Watts reworked the ideas of the Psalms to provide a Christocentric interpretation.[57] And, following him, the Wesley brothers rejected the rationed sensuality of the English Psalter. John Wesley (1703-1791) mocked the music of the English Psalter, much preferring the worship of the Methodists who:

> sing praise to God ... with the spirit, and with the understanding also: not in the miserable, scandalous doggerel of Hopkins and Sternhold [i.e. the English Psalter], but in psalms and hymns which are both sense and poetry.[58]

---

52 Vajta, *Luther on Worship*, 156.
53 Vajta, *Luther on Worship*, 158.
54 Evans, *Music in the Modern Church* 32.
55 Cited in Evans, *Music in the Modern Church* 32
56 Evans, *Music in the Modern Church*, 31.
57 Flynn, 'Liturgical Music', 784.
58 John Wesley, 'To A Friend, On Public Worship', in *The Works of the Rev John Wesley: Tracts and Letters on Various Subjects* (1st ed.; New York: J & J Harper, 1827), 233.

Wesley saw no need to insist on simple harmony, approving of whatever 'may best raise the soul to God'.[59] He also favoured communal singing over professionalism, desiring 'well-composed and well-adapted tunes' sung 'not by a handful of wild unawakened striplings, but by a whole serious congregation … all standing before God, and praising him lustily and with a good courage.'[60] His Arminianism made provoking spiritual response all the more urgent: for Wesley the goal was not simply to *express* emotion, but to *direct* it, using the power of music to cut people to the heart and bring religious revival.[61]

Reacting against the established church, these non-conformist hymn writers valued cultural relevance over traditional forms, emotional engagement over solemnity, and clear biblical teaching over literal words of scripture. They set a trajectory for worship music theology in many traditions in the nineteenth and twentieth centuries.[62] The Victorian Church of England produced many notable hymn writers, while North American folk 'gospel songs' spread worldwide, often on the back of evangelistic missions.[63] The twentieth century, however, was marked by a new crossover from secular culture. Born, it is often said, in Calvary Chapel California, the 'Praise and Worship' genre went international, largely propelled by Pentecostal churches.[64]

---

[59] John Wesley, 'To A Friend, On Public Worship', in **The Works of the Rev John Wesley: Tracts and Letters on Various Subjects** (1st ed.; New York: J & J Harper, 1827), 233.
[60] John Wesley, 'To A Friend, On Public Worship', in **The Works of the Rev John Wesley: Tracts and Letters on Various Subjects** (1st ed.; New York: J & J Harper, 1827), 233.
[61] Evans, **Music in the Modern Church,** 34. For an excellent modern discussion on emotion in music see Jeremy Begbie, **Resounding Truth: Christian Wisdom in the World of Music** (Grand Rapids: Baker Academic, 2007), 302.
[62] Non-conformist hymn writers are well represented in the twentieth century **Australian Hymn Book with Catholic Supplement** (Sydney: Collins, 1977).
[63] Evans, **Music in the Modern Church**, 37.
[64] Evans, **Music in the Modern Church**, 39.

www.ingramcontent.com/pod-product-compliance
Lightning Source LLC
Chambersburg PA
CBHW070631300426
44113CB00010B/1735